THE TURNAROUND

Union Planters downtown bank building today

THE TURNAROUND

by

John J. Pepin

Western Heritage Books, Inc.
Oklahoma City   1980

Copyright © 1980
John J. Pepin

Manufactured in the United States of America

ISBN: 0-86546-014-0

TO JOYCE, LAURA, AND LYNN

Special recognition and thanks are given to Messrs. William
M. Matthews, Jr., James A. Gurley, and Robert M. Johnson
for their contributions to this book.

PREFACE .

Two years ago the former business editor of the Memphis *Commercial Appeal* published an article in the *American Banker* referring to one of the most interesting and educational business dramas of recent times:

> During the depths of the 1973-75 recession, one bank, the $772.7 million-deposit Union Planters National Bank of Memphis, suffered a series of financial shocks the equivalent of the severest that struck anywhere in the nation's banking system.
>
> Coupled with the bank's business setbacks were scores of instances of employee and customer dishonesty that eventually resulted in 11 former employees and 30 outsiders being indicted by a Federal grand jury. Substantially all of those indicted have either admitted or been convicted of crimes against the bank, and several are in prison today.
>
> Despite its immense difficulties, Union Planters, a one-bank holding company, staved off collapse during a period when the failures of U.S. National Bank of San Diego, Franklin National Bank of New York and Hamilton National Bank of Chattanooga clearly demonstrated the vulnerability of all financial institutions.[1]

The year 1980 threatens again to demonstrate the vulnerability of financial institutions to severe economic instability, as prospective bank failures are in the news once more.

This book has been written for business executives, government leaders and interested students of business. It describes the evolution of events, managerial philosophies, miscalculated strategies and inadequate controls which brought Union Planters to near-collapse. The book further portrays the problems/struggles encountered and the strategies formulated and implemented by management in its fight to keep the 109-year-old bank's doors open.

Union Planters National Bank returned to a profitable operating status at the end of its 1977 fiscal year, evidencing the "turn-around." It is the author's sincere desire that the lessons to be learned from this delineation of the successful rise, near-demise, and turnaround of one of the largest banks in the South will provide a background that will prove meaningful to its readers.

Memphis, Tennessee   JOHN J. PEPIN
June 1, 1980

CONTENTS

ILLUSTRATIONS

THE TURNAROUND

1
THE EARLY YEARS

In order fully to appreciate the evolving events and managerial philosophies which brought about the catastrophic problems that beset Union Planters' management in 1974, one must understand the objectives of prior management, as well as how the organization was structured to achieve those goals. A summary of the bank's operations in the early years of its existence points out the immediate successes enjoyed by the institution's management and the impact of its early leaders on the firm:

> . . . [T]he bank traces its ancestry back to the DeSoto Insurance and Banking Co. which was chartered by the Tennessee Legislature in 1857 and did a general insurance and banking business until 1869, when its affairs were taken over by the Union & Planters Bank.
> In those days home insurance companies were strong, did a big business and were really the backbone of finance in the South. Trust companies as a rule were included, and had a wide latitude. They were financial agents for their customers, for then it was more difficult to obtain a charter for a bank than for an insurance and trust company.[2]

During 1869 the company received permission from the Tennessee legislature "to discontinue the business of Insurance and adopt the Banking business whenever so decided by a vote of the stockholders."[3] William M. Farrington, president of the insurance company, then called a meeting of the stockholders to amend its charter and to

Samuel P. Read, one of the organizers of Union & Planters Bank of Memphis and its first cashier, succeeding to the presidency in 1897. (The Story of a Memphis Institution).

enter the banking business under the name of the Union and Planters Bank of Memphis. The name Union and Planters Bank of Memphis was chosen to honor branches of two Nashville banks, the Union Bank and the Planters Bank. These two branches had served Memphis for 20 years, but in 1862 they had elected to move to another city when Federal troops advanced on Memphis.

Capitalized at $600,000, the Union and Planters Bank of Memphis began operations on September 1, 1869. Farrington retained the presidency of the firm. From its beginning the bank prospered, and in June of

1870 (with less than one year of operations) a six percent dividend was declared for its stockholders. The bank continued to prosper for the next three years, but its prosperity was threatened in 1873 when Memphis suffered an epidemic of yellow fever which killed 2000 people. "And as if that was not enough, a financial panic struck the country at the same time, terrible in its effects. September 19, 1873, is alluded to in the histories as 'Black Friday.' But altho other banks suspended business, the Union & Planters Bank remained open."[4]

To convince the people of the safety of their deposits during the Panic of 1873, S. P. Read, the bank's Cashier (who would become its president in 1897), "threw open his doors and piled the money high, assuring the people that the money they had entrusted to his bank was subject to their demand and that all depositors would be paid dollar for dollar in 'coin of the realm' for every demand they had against the bank."[5]

Following the bank's survival of the Panic of 1873, a surprising event occurred: William M. Farrington, the founding president and one of the bank's largest stockholders, was not reappointed to his position by the board of directors. This action stemmed from recognition that Farrington personally had borrowed (either individually or through joint indebtedness in the form of several loans) the sum of $203,991.97 from the Union and Planters Bank, approximately one-third of its available capital. Farrington, astounded at the appointment of C. W. Goyer to the presidency of the bank on January 14, 1874, published a 23-page pamphlet on September 26, 1874, *Address to the Stockholders of the Union & Planters Bank of Memphis*. In this, Farrington cited several interesting points which provide insight into his thinking:

> The astonishment expressed by stockholders, customers, clerks and officers of other banks at the result (appointment of a new president), illustrates the secrecy of the plot, and the further fact that the change was

William M. Farrington, first president of the bank. (The Story of a Memphis Institution).

neither desired or expected by the community . . . . It will be seen that I had full power to elect any board that I desired, and it is not necessary to disguise the fact that those chosen owe their election to me. I had secured the charter, procured the subscription of stock, organized the bank, was one of its largest stockholders, and had been president since its organization.

. . . This brings me to the debt which I owed the bank. . . . [T]he amount has been magnified into proportions far beyond the reality—but whether the amount was great or small, the debt has been paid, principal and interest, except about five hundred and seventy-two dollars, which was tendered and refused [refers to Mr. Farrington's individual debt] . . . .

. . . Mr. Greenlaw and myself owed the bank jointly, a very large debt . . . but, I doubt if you were told that it had been regularly passed upon by the discount committee from time to time, read out to the directors, and approved by them. I doubt, also, if you were told, with these loans, collaterals were pledged, which were satisfactory at the time, and when additional collaterals were required they also were furnished.

. . . Knowing that I would be absent when the note would fall due, Mr. Greenlaw went before the board two or three days in advance of the maturity, represented the fact of my absence, and that arrangements were on foot to pay off the note, perhaps, in a few days, and expressed the wish that it would be held up accordingly. He was afterwards informed that it had been referred to the regular discount committee which meets daily. When I returned home I found rumors all over the city that our note had been protested.

. . . If you recollect what I have stated, you will see that I have paid over one hundred thousand dollars in cash in about four months to the bank. If actions have any meaning it seems that every payment that has been made has had the effect to exasperate certain parties, and cause them to resort to more unscrupulous efforts to injure my credit. My collaterals, pledged for the payment of debts, had been transferred without necessity; my note protested when there were no indorsers to bind; my private indebtedness to the bank exhibited to parties who had no interest in the stock or management of the bank; my private fortune and character discussed in public and private places with a view to injure me, and now to have the threat cast in my teeth, that my collaterals would be sold, seemed but additional evidence of a determination to strike another blow at "my good name," and to bring dis-

credit upon a character that I had been a life time in
striking to build up . . . .

But, I have drawn from this experience a lesson
that, I trust, will be of service both to the bank and
myself, and it is this: I am satisfied no officer, under
any circumstances, should be permitted to borrow a
dollar from the bank with which he is connected.
Loans to me passed through the same ordeal, and at
the same rate of interest as to others, and have been a
source of profit to the bank; but, through malice or a
want of discretion, (perhaps both,) a publicity has been
given to them, causing discussion and criticism that
have been injurious to the bank as well as myself . . . .

I presume it will not be considered vanity upon my
part, to assume that many of you were influenced to
make your investment in the stock of the bank through
my agency. I congratulate you, as well as myself, that I
have never lost sight of your interest, or of my first
desire to make the bank a source of pride as well as
profit to every one connected with its management or
interested in its stock.[6]

On October 8, 1874, the Union and Planters Bank
responded to Farrington's pamphlet by issuing a lengthy
statement to the stockholders noting inconsistencies in
the former president's document. The final paragraph
of the statement summarized the bank's rebuttal: "In
electing Mr. Goyer President of the Union and Planters
Bank instead of Mr. Farrington, we have simply carried
out an imperative duty to our stockholders and to
ourselves."[7]

An economic result of the yellow fever epidemic that
struck Memphis was the migration of numerous survi-
vors to other areas, leaving the City and the State in
financial difficulties. During the next few years, efforts
were made to revitalize the City. Then, in the summer of
1878, yellow fever returned. In Colonel James M. Keat-
ing's *History of Memphis*, the yellow fever epidemic of

1878 is referred to as "the horror of the century, the most soul-harrowing episode in the history of the English-speaking people in America . . . . All who could had fled and all were in camp who would go."[8] "Out of a population reduced to 19,500 (a significant decrease from the Federal Census of 1870 population estimate of 40,226 inhabitants) by the hegira from the city following the plague and panic of 1873, there was a total of 17,600 cases and a mortality of 5150."[9] Despite these horrible circumstances, employees of the Union and Planters Bank completed their daily tasks and enabled the bank to establish its reputation of "having been open every business day since 1869."[10]

Following the yellow fever epidemic of 1878, Memphis became recognized for its natural advantages, including geographic location, surrounding forests and fertile soil. In 1881, Goyer's successor, A. C. Treadwell, became the president of the Union and Planters Bank "and served until 1885, when ill health compelled him to retire."[11] Napoleon Hill, "one of the biggest cotton dealers in the South, heading the firm of Hill, Fontaine & Co.",[12] succeeded Treadwell. The Union and Planters Bank continued to grow and on December 31, 1885, "disclosed total deposits of $1,041,000, Capital Surplus and Profits, $755,000, and Cash and Exchange, $386,000."[13]

In 1897, one of the organizers of the company and its first cashier, Samuel P. Read, became president of the Union and Planters Bank. Read was an aggressive manager who would serve as president until his death in February of 1915. "To the public, 'Mr. Read's bank' was like Gibraltar, a tower of financial strength and integrity, in which unstinted confidence could be reposed."[14] During his tenure as president, Read evidently put into practice his most favored saying, "Eternal vigilance is the price that we must pay for our own security,"[15] as he led

Napoleon Hill, president 1885-1897. (The Story of a Memphis Institution).

the bank through two financial panics. Under Reed's leadership the Tennessee Trust Company and the Union and Planters Bank of Memphis consolidated in 1906, with the bank operating under the new title Union & Planters Bank & Trust Company. New quarters were occupied in the 81 Madison Building, and the bank had aggregate resources of $6,694,660.

In 1907, Memphis banks survived a panic caused by a scarcity of funds. The minutes of the Memphis Clearing House (an organization of Memphis bankers formed as a means of settling the daily accounts between member banks arising from their banking operations) indicate that on October 29, 1907, "many meetings were held relating to the money panic and the issuance of Clearing-House Certificates in lieu of paper money. Some banks put into circulation large amounts of their own cashier's checks. During that panic, no cash was paid out and no customers were given credit for any checks on any out-of-town points. Then the minutes show the waning of this panic."[16]

Due to disruptions in Europe, another panic followed in 1914. Repeated financial panics over the previous 20 years had led to the founding of the Federal Reserve System as World War I began. Read, still practicing his philosophy of "eternal vigilance" at 83 years of age, capably led the bank through the troubled period. On February 8, 1915, two days before his 84th birthday, Read died.

Frank F. Hill, the son of Union & Planters' former president Napoleon Hill, was chosen to succeed Read. Hill "met his enlarged responsibilities and opportunities with enthusiasm and close application. Immediately he undertook to put into practice his cherished ideals. From the beginning of his incumbency, the bank took on new life, and its deposits mounted. To a conservative policy which gave the bank a strong standing, he added the vigor of young blood, enterprise, aggressiveness, and modern ideas. The bank was improved, not only in physical appearance, equipment, and organization for service, but also in its 'spirit of *noblesse oblige*,' rank imposes obligation,' was made of emphatic policy . . . . Under Mr. Hill's leadership, within the few years of his administration, the bank has surpassed all previous records in the South for comparative growth."[17]

When Frank Hill became the president of the bank in 1915, total deposits were approximately $5,000,000 and total resources approached $7,400,000.[18] Hill began the

movement for establishing a Federal Reserve branch in
Memphis; and, in October of 1917, Union and Planters
Bank and Trust Company became the first state bank in
Tennessee to join the Federal Reserve System.[19] In
February of 1918 the Mercantile National Bank was ab-
sorbed in a merger, thereby increasing deposits of the
Union and Planters Bank and Trust Company to
$19,584,000, and total resources to $28,479,000.[20]

In 1919, the Union and Planters Bank and Trust
Company was the largest bank in Memphis, and one of
the largest banks in the South. Under the Hill administration, the bank began a branch banking strategy by
acquiring the North Memphis Savings Bank. In 1924,
the Bank consolidated with the Guaranty Bank and
Trust Company of Memphis and relocated to 67 Madison Avenue at Front Street. During that year, Mr. Hill
was succeeded by Frank Hayden as president of the
Union and Planters Bank and Trust Company.

Mr. Hayden was the president of the bank during the
years 1924-1929. The bank continued to grow, survived
a "bank run" in 1928, but was then reorganized by an
early conglomerate in a way that threatened its destruc-
tion. The bank was saved from possible disaster when it
became a national bank on July 9, 1929. Receipt of the
national charter, plus the insistence of some of the bank's
directors that the Comptroller of the Currency protect it
from being abused by Caldwell and Company ("the
largest banking house ever before established in the
South."[21], insured the continued viability of Union
Planters. By contrast, however, the episode "can be regarded as an important factor in the downfall of
Caldwell & Company."[22]

Caldwell and Company was:

> . . . The largest banking house ever before estab-
> lished in the South, whose financial misfeasance dur-
> ing the prosperous twenties led to its eventual collapse
> and brought ruin to numerous innocent investors.

Caldwell and Company was founded in Nashville in 1917 by Rogers Caldwell, the son of a leading local banker and businessman. Beginning as a small underwriter and distributor of Southern municipal bonds, the firm soon branched out into real estate bonds and industrial securities as well. Control of important banks in Tennessee and Arkansas was acquired; newspapers, and even Nashville's professional baseball team, came under the firm's ownership. Caldwell and Company was, truly, a pioneer conglomerate.

Caldwell and Company also ventured into the realm of politics, supporting certain politicians (notably Colonel Luke Lea) with questionable benefits accruing to the firm, including substantial state deposits in Caldwell's Bank of Tennessee.

In November 1930 the firm went into receivership. Unethical practices, including overextension in the acquisition of banks, insurance companies, and other business, had already strained Caldwell and Company's assets. With the 1929 collapse of stock prices, Rogers Caldwell could not meet the company's obligations, and he began to squeeze all available cash from the various controlled firms . . . . Even the aforementioned State of Tennessee deposits, which helped float his empire for a while, could not prevent its collapse—a collapse which resulted in a multimillion-dollar loss to Tennessee's Treasury, public hysteria, and clamor for the impeachment of the Governor of Tennessee. . . .

The extension of Caldwell and Company's banking interests into Memphis, Tennessee, placed it in a strategic position with regard to the banking systems in three of the four largest cities of the state, thus enabling it to become by far the strongest influence in Tennessee banking. Caldwell and Company entered Memphis banking in May, 1928, when Rogers Caldwell for his company, Luke Lea for himself, and Edward Potter, Jr., for the Commerce-Union Company, the security affiliate of the Commerce-Union Bank of Nashville, purchased 751 shares, or 51 per cent, of the capital stock of the Manhattan Savings Bank and Trust

Company, from the heirs of I. Samelson, thus gaining control of the bank. The group paid $400 a share, or a total of $300,400, for the stock, borrowing the funds from the National Park Bank of New York. The Manhattan Bank was considered the strongest small bank in the city. It had had a long and profitable existence and its stock was regarded as a desirable investment. At the close of 1928 it had deposits of $8,613,000 and assets of $9,866,000.[23]

Two months after Caldwell and Company took over the Manhattan Bank, a "run" occurred in Memphis. The manner in which Hayden stopped the run at Union and Planters was described by a vice president and cashier of the bank at the time:

Mr. Shepherd was on the bank's staff July 6, 1928, when a run—started strictly by rumor—began on the city's banks. Of course, the lobbies soon were filled with customers anxious to withdraw their funds. Union Planters, Mr. Shepherd said, built up a considerable cash balance at the Memphis Branch of the St. Louis Federal Reserve Bank by wiring in money from its correspondent banks. Frank Hayden, then president of Union Planters, ordered cold drinks served to customers as they waited in line to get their money. He also climbed on top of a desk in the lobby and announced that the bank had plenty of money and that it would remain open as long as necessary. This announcement had the desired effect, and many left without taking out their money, while others redeposited the money they had withdrawn. Bookkeeping department personnel worked most of the night posting deposits on hand-operated bookkeeping machines.

The rumor persisted the next day, July 7, and the lobby of the bank's North Memphis Branch was soon crowded. Money was rushed from the Main Office, and Mr. Hayden instructed the tellers to pile the cash high in their individual cages so that it was in plain view. The sight of thousands of dollars in each cage had a calming effect, and most of the customers decided against withdrawing their money.

By July 10, said Mr. Shepherd, bank officials decided the run was over, and they began reducing the cash on hand. As cashier, he signed a check for $2.5 million made out to the Fed [Federal Reserve] to cover the wire transfer of the money back to Union Planters' correspondent banks.[24]

However, the incident provided an opportunity for Caldwell and Company to further its ambitious plans in Memphis:

Not content with the control of a small bank in the city, the group sought a larger one . . . . [T]he Union and Planters Bank and Trust Company . . . came through the one-day run unharmed. But basically the bank was in a rather unsound condition because of its large volume of slow and doubtful assets and a thorough reorganization was desirable. Knowing that this condition existed, the men who had bought control of the Manhattan together with two Memphis bankers, Frank Hayden, who was already connected with the bank, and William White, executive vice president of the Manhattan, offered to reorganize the Union and Planters with a view toward improving its condition. The offer was accepted and shortly after the undertaking was begun, James E. Caldwell, through the Fourth and First National Company, was asked to join the group, which he did. To carry out the transaction, Rogers Caldwell, James E. Caldwell, Luke Lea, and Edward Potter, Jr., of Nashville, and William White and Frank Hayden of Memphis established the Bank Securities Corporation on February 25, 1929, with capital stock of $12,000, represented by 120 shares of par value $100, 20 shares of which went to each of the six in the group.

The reorganization plan of the Union and Planters called for increasing the capital of the bank from

$2,500,000 to $3,500,000, the surplus from $200,000 to $3,500,000, and undivided profits from approximately $830,000 to $1,750,000, while slow and doubtful assets totaling $1,700,000 were to be removed and replaced by cash. The Manhattan Bank was to become an affiliated institution of the Union and Planters with all of the Manhattan stock trusteed for the stockholders of the larger bank. The capital of the Manhattan was to be increased from $150,000 to $700,000, surplus to $700,000, and undivided profits to $1,050,000. Finally, the new bank was to apply for a Federal charter and, until this was granted, it was to operate as the Union Planters Bank and Trust Company, thus dropping the first "and" from its former title.

Under the reorganization plan approximately $5,220,000 was needed to increase the net worth items of the Union and Planters Bank, $1,450,000 for the same purpose in the Manhattan Bank, and $1,700,000 to replace the assets to be removed from the Union and Planters, thus making a total cash requirement of approximately $8,370,000 which the reorganization group expected to raise by the sale of Union Planters stock. The par value of the stock in the new bank was set at $10, in place of the old par of $100, and the stockholders of Union and Planters Bank were given the option of selling their old stocks at $250 a share or exchanging it for new stock. There were 115,000 out of a total of 350,000 shares of stock of the new bank thus offered, while the stockholders of the Manhattan were given the privilege of exchanging their stock for 14,000 shares of the new bank. In all, 129,000 shares of the new Union Planters Bank were offered in exchange for the shares of the old Union and Planters Bank and the Manhattan Bank.

The old stockholders expressed their approval of the plan by taking almost all the stock offered them, thus requiring a negligible cash payment to them. Of the remaining 221,000 shares, Bank Securities Cor-

poration was to hold 75,000 as its permanent investment while 146,000 shares were offered to the public
at $63 a share early in 1929 by Caldwell and Company,
Fourth and First National Company, and Commerce-
Union Company in Nashville, and by Union and Planters Company and Manhattan Securities Company in
Memphis. The sale of all of this stock would have
raised $9,198,000, which would have been sufficient
to carry through reorganization, and to give to the
promoting group a cash profit of over $800,000 and
the $1,700,000 of slow assets to be removed from the
bank, at the same time allowing the group to retain
enough stock to control the bank.

The Union and Planters stock was not absorbed in
the market as readily as anticipated, some 109,000
shares having been sold by February 28, 1929, the date
set for the reorganization, rather than the 146,000
expected. This was learned only after the Nashville
group, headed by James E. Caldwell and Luke Lea,
had reached Memphis to conclude the deal, and the
necessity of obtaining $700,000 was pressing. This
obstacle was overcome by the Bank of Tennessee's
advancing the needed amount, this action being taken
by T. G. Donovan, who came to supervise the details of
the transaction. The actual transfer of funds to the
credit of the Union Planters Bank was made by Donovan's giving the bank duplicate deposit slips on the
Bank of Tennessee, Fourth and First National Bank,
and Commerce-Union Bank. Had the representatives
of the old bank asked that checks be given rather than
deposit slips, as they could and probably should have
done, the whole deal might have fallen through for
Donovan had no power to sign checks for the various
banks and the Bank of Tennessee was in no position to
honor the checks that would have been drawn on it
without first borrowing from other sources. But no
questions were asked and the deal was completed.

The new Union Planters Bank and Trust Company

was a materially improved institution after its reorganization. The paying in of cash to increase its net worth and to replace its $1,700,000 of doubtful assets had placed it in a very sound condition. Frank Hayden, a leading Memphis banker who had taken part in the reorganization, was made president while William White remained as executive vice president of the Manhattan Savings Bank, the wholly owned affiliate of the Union Planters Bank. At the close of 1929 Union Planters had total assets of $38,537,000 while the Manhattan had assets of $10,830,000, the two combined constituting by far the largest banking group in the city.

As soon as the new bank was organized Caldwell and Company began seeking funds from it. In fact, on the way back to Nashville, after buying the bank, Donovan persuaded Luke Lea that the Bank of Tennessee should be rewarded for its services by a deposit from Union Planters of $500,000, which amount was immediately transferred by wire. By June 30, 1929, this deposit had been reduced to $238,000 but the Manhattan Bank had on deposit at that time with the Bank of Tennessee $605,000, making a total unsecured deposit of $843,000. At the same date Caldwell and Company had sold $616,000 of notes and bonds under a repurchase agreement to the Union Planters and $259,000 to the Manhattan, or a total of $875,000 to the two banks. Further, the Union Planters Bank had loaned Caldwell and Company $720,000 of Memphis, Tennessee, Revenue Anticipation Notes which Caldwell and Company used to secure several of its deposit accounts. Thus, in all, the two Memphis banks were advancing Caldwell and Company the astoundingly large sum of $2,438,000 as of June 30, 1929, four months after the reorganization had been completed.

Certain of the Memphis directors of the bank soon became concerned lest the new owners after placing it on a sound basis would proceed virtually to wreck it. Their opportunity to protect the bank came when it secured a national charter on July 9, 1929, and became the Union Planters National Bank and Trust Company. These directors insisted that the Comptroller of the Currency exercise his power to protect the bank, which led to the agreement contained in the following letter:

MEMPHIS, TENNESSEE
April 9, 1929

COMPTROLLER OF THE CURRENCY
WASHINGTON, D.C.

DEAR SIR:

In a meeting held in Memphis, Tennessee, with your examiners, Wm. R. Young and John S. Wood, the matter of the application of the Union Planters Bank and Trust Company to convert into a national bank was discussed at length and in detail. The five undersigned, Rogers Caldwell, Luke Lea, Edward Potter, Jr., Frank Hayden and William White, are members of a group that underwrote the reorganization of Union Planters Bank and Trust Company.

After a full discussion of the matter, the undersigned expressed the opinion that in view of their large stock interest in Union Planters Bank and Trust Company it would be to the interest of the bank that they would not jointly, nor severally, nor individually, nor any of their corporations, firms, enterprises or underwritings either directly or indirectly, by accommodation loans or otherwise use any of the funds of the proposed Union Planters National Bank and Trust Company or the Manhattan Savings Bank and Trust Company; and it is further provided and agreed that if on the date of the conversion of the Union Planters Bank and Trust Company into a national bank the said Rogers Caldwell, Luke Lea, Edward Potter, Jr., Frank Hayden, or William White, or either of them, jointly or severally, individually, or through any of their corporations, firms, enterprises or underwritings, directly or indirectly owe the Union Planters Bank and Trust Company or the Manhattan Savings Bank and Trust Company, or both, that all of the said indebtedness will be paid within six months from the date said Union Planters Bank and Trust Company converts into a national bank.

This agreement on the part of the undersigned is to remain in full force and effect until modified or abrogated by the Comptroller of the Currency.

Respectfully,

ROGERS CALDWELL
LUKE LEA
EDWARD POTTER, JR.
FRANK HAYDEN
WILLIAM WHITE

Thus, the Union Planters National Bank and Trust Company was rendered of little use to Caldwell and Company as a source of funds and the investment house was faced with the necessity of repaying the advances the bank had already made.

Moreover, the transaction necessitated the raising of large amounts of cash to carry the investment in the stock of Union Planters National Bank. Bank Securities Corporation, after the promotion had been completed, owned 131,396 shares of Union Planters stock which it carried at its cost of $2,342,000, including payment of $50,000 to L. K. Saulsbury of Memphis, who had acted as agent for the group. The remainder of its assets were primarily the $1,700,000 of slow and doubtful assets taken from the Union Planters Bank. To liquidate these assets, a subsidiary, the West Tennessee Company, was organized, its entire stock being owned by Bank Securities Corporation, and some progress was made toward realizing on this property. The funds obtained from this source were used to replenish the reserves for accrued interest and taxes of the two banks which had been added to surplus when the reorganization took place and also to buy out the interests of Hayden and White in the undertaking. Hayden was let out as president of the bank in October, 1929, and his stock in Bank Securities Corporation was bought from him by the holding company and retired. White then became president, but in July, 1930, he was removed, his stock of Bank Securities Corporation bought and retired, and an outsider, E. P. Peacock of Clarksdale, Mississippi, was selected to head the bank.

At the close of 1929 Bank Securities Corporation owed a total of $4,288,000, which was secured by its stock in Union Planters National Bank. Its holding of this stock had increased as a result of efforts to peg the price which could be financed only by additional borrowings. Of its total debts $2,045,000 was owed to Caldwell and Company and the Bank of Tennessee, which meant that Caldwell and Company had had to borrow from some other sources to provide these sums. Bank Securities borrowed the remaining funds from other Nashville banks as well as from New York banks. Thus, by the end of 1929 the promotion had become exceedingly burdensome to Caldwell and Company. It was having to borrow large sums in an effort to maintain a market for Union Planters stock, and other banks which would lend money directly to Caldwell and Company were advancing funds to Bank

Securities Corporation, thus reducing the amount of
funds Caldwell and Company could expect to borrow
from them, while at the same time it was precluded
from borrowing from the Memphis banks by the
agreement with the Comptroller of the Currency.
There was in all about $4,500,000 locked up in the
stock of Union Planters National Bank that might
otherwise have been available to Caldwell and Company. As the financial condition of the investment
house became steadily weaker, the need for these
funds was felt very strongly. Thus in many respects the
Union Planters transaction can be regarded as an important factor in the downfall of Caldwell and
Company.[25]

The Caldwell and Company era at Union Planters
was brought to a close by Ed. P. Peacock, who followed
Hayden and White as president. Peacock had organized
the Bank of Clarksdale, Mississippi, in 1900, and was its
president in 1930 when he also was elected to the presidency of Union Planters. Four months later, the Cald-
wells resigned their directorships of the Union Planters
and Manhattan banks, and their influence on each bank
diminished. The following is an account from a newspaper article dated November 15, 1930:

Edward P. Peacock, president of the Union Planters
National Bank & Trust Co., and of the Manhattan
Savings Bank & Trust Co., announced yesterday that
James E. Caldwell and his son, Meredith Caldwell,
both of Nashville, have resigned as directors of the two
institutions, and that their resignations had been
accepted.

Board of Directors in session. (The Story of a Memphis Institution).

These resignations sever all connections between these banks and the Caldwell interests of Nashville. It was announced several days ago that neither Rogers Caldwell, nor Caldwell & Co., nor any of the companies controlled by Caldwell & Co., were indebted in any sum to either the Union Planters or the Manhattan.

The control and administration (but not the sole ownership) of these banks are now wholly in the hands of officers and directors who are residents of Memphis.[26]

In 1932, Peacock returned to Clarksdale. Gilmer Winston, a long-time employee and senior executive of Union Planters National Bank and Trust Company, then became the bank's president.

In March of 1933, Union Planters absorbed the Manhattan Savings Bank, and began operating it as Union Planters' second branch:

> . . . These moves by which the Manhattan Bank becomes part of the Union Planters Bank are in line with the proclamation of President Roosevelt, a joint announcement by Mr. Winston and Mr. Tefft said. They are also in pursuit of a policy decided upon some time ago.
>
> It means that the Union Planters Bank will confine its business solely to banking. This is the solution to the present national situation as outlined by the president's proclamation and the regulations of the secretary of the treasury.
>
> Under the plan, the Union Planters guarantees the deposits of the Manhattan and brings them under the protection of the national banking laws. The depositors will have all the security and protection of the Union Planters, and the Union Planters will have the added assets of the Manhattan behind it.[27]

During April of 1933 the board of directors of Union Planters was reorganized. Winston became chairman of the board of directors, and Vance Alexander, a Nashville banker, succeeded Winston as president. "When Mr. Alexander took charge on April 8, 1933, the bank's deposits totaled $26,879,926.90 and its capital structure was approximately $5,200,000."[28] A newspaper account of the board's reorganization stated:

> Col. Walter Canada's plan for reorganizing the board of directors of Union Planters National Bank & Co., went thru without a hitch Saturday morning.

Col. Canada was elected general counsel and a group of his friends were elected to the board.

They immediately named Gilmer Winston chairman of the board; Vance Alexander, of Nashville, president; and Edward C. Tefft, first vice president.[29]

Under Alexander's leadership, a new era was introduced to the bank.

2
FOCUSING ON AGRICULTURE LOANS

Vance J. Alexander was executive vice president of the American National Bank in Nashville when at age 60 he became president of Union Planters. For various reasons, Union Planters had just experienced three corporate helmsmen—White, Peacock, and Winston—in the previous four years (1929-33), and was in the process of reorganizing itself. Furthermore, like the entire United States business community, Union Planters was attempting to deal with the effects of the Great Depression. The leadership, optimism and lending strategy that Alexander brought to Union Planters proved timely, correct, and important to the growth of the firm.

The optimistic lending strategy implemented by Alexander was described in the November 1934 issue of a prominent banking journal, *Burroughs Clearing House*. Alexander reportedly "urged bankers to remove their 'deep blue glasses' in considering applications for loans from businessmen."[30] The article and the reasoning leading to Alexander's strategy were summarized in a now worn and yellowed newspaper clipping preserved in the bank's archives. In that story, Alexander explained:

> The loan applicant who can come into his bank today and put up a good argument for a loan is prima facie a better risk than the man who could come in six years ago and demand accommodations on the strength of a glorious financial statement . . . .[T]he bank customer who has kept himself going and making a little progress stands an extraordinarily good

*Vance J. Alexander, President of Union Planters National
Bank 1933-1952.*

chance of becoming one of the leaders in his line of
business, profession or industry during the years
ahead.

As such, he becomes the best possible type of bank
customer. It seems obviously sound policy for the
banker with an eye for the future to earn the continuing allegiance of this class of man by giving him the
benefit of the doubt now when credit is scarce.[31]

However, Alexander also cautioned against "intemperate and inexperienced advocates of unsound expansion of credits, lest we blind ourselves to the sane, conservative openings which all of us wish for and need."[32]

During 1935, one local director of Union Planters purchased 10,000 shares of the bank's stock at $22.50 per share from the Commerce-Union Bank of Nashville. In 1936, more than 40,000 additional shares of Union Planters stock were purchased from Nashville interests at $32 per share. The result of these transactions was that controlling ownership in Union Planters was regained by local investors.[33]

Insight into the agricultural emphasis of Alexander's loan strategy during this period is found in a typewritten paper (also yellowed and located in the basement archives of the bank) in which Alexander is quoted as forecasting an improved economy and tremendous growth potential for Memphis and the Mid-South during 1936 and future years:

> Any Southerner is making a mistake today by migrating to another section of the country thinking that it offers better business possibilities than his own native Dixie.
>
> I say this because the Southern horizon is as bright with opportunity now as was that of the far West when Mr. Greely made his now famous remark. There has been in the more recent past and there is now, every indication that our section is steadily and surely forging to the fore. We are in a period of economic transition industrially as well as agriculturally.
>
> Let's look at the latter, agriculture, which is, after all, the very backbone of Dixie. Our farmers have learned in the past few years the wisdom, more than that, the necessity of raising more than one money crop . . . . They have also learned in the school of experience that it is to their decided advantage to plant not only the so-called money crops, but food for their families

and feed for their stock. These lessons, dearly learned though some of them were, cannot and will not soon be forgotten. It is estimated on good authority that the South's farm income for 1936 will reach $2,835,821,000, for a gain over 1935 of $360,315,000.

Another basic reason for predicting continuing and increasingly favorable agricultural conditions is the steady rise in farm land values which is the natural result of better prices on farm products. Thus, the cycle completes itself . . . .

So much for agriculture in general. Now let's look specifically at the South's greatest crop—cotton. World stocks of raw cotton have dropped six million bales from the seventeen million bale peak four years ago. The narrowing of the price spread between U.S. and foreign growths has brought a sharp upturn in export. . . . And home consumption of our own cotton is constantly growing.

Raising an annual average of 36% of the world's crop of this great commodity, our Mid-South states are this year, even more than usually fortunate in that they benefited by ideal climatic conditions while other cotton territories were adversely affected . . . . At present price levels this means an income of approximately $292,740,000 for this section.

Localizing the subject a bit, it is well for Memphis to remember that on the basis of previous figures, approximately 16%, or 1,857,440 bales will move through the cotton marts of the Bluff City alone. That means an estimated $130,020,800 for our immediate surrounding territory . . . .

Through modern laboratory research, cotton seed, once burned as trash, has become one of the most useful of all our agricultural products. Memphis is the cotton seed capital of the world—a central gathering point of millions of tons of Mid-South cotton seeds . . . .

As to the Mid-South's agriculture future, I share the opinion of many of our foremost authorities—that is,

that our Southland will continue to progress agricul-
turally so long as its farmers remember the lessons of
the past and avoid the overproductions which are the
inevitable predecessors of any drastic collapse in farm
prices.

The Mid-South's industrial possibilities for the future are another source of satisfaction. Our wealth of
natural resources, the proximity of raw materials,
plentiful labor at low cost, with minimum likelihood of
agitation, and comparatively low tax rates, all combine
to lend powerful influence to the movement South-
ward of many branches of the nation's industries.
Many of these businesses have already established fac-
tories, branch offices and distribution points . . . .

Outstanding commercial loans are one of the surest
evidences of expansion and prosperity. Memphis
banks have registered a fair increase in these loans,
while the deposits of correspondent banks with Memphis financial institutions have also shown substantial
gains . . . .

But we don't have to study cold facts and figures to
realize the extent of our business betterment. Every
day our shopping districts are crowded with buyers.
The happy smile of returning prosperity has replaced
the gloomy frown of depression on the countenance of
the Mid-South. We have come far in the past few years
and from any and every angle from which we consider
it, we are going further.[34]

The growth predicted by Alexander for Memphis
benefited Union Planters: "As of December 30, 1939,
deposits of $77,957,817 were the highest ever published
by a bank in the mid-south."[35] According to rankings
published by *American Banker* magazine, Union Planters
by 1939 had become the 97th largest bank in the country
in terms of deposits, and by the close of 1940 ranked 96th
among the nation's 100 largest banks with deposits of
$89,350,765.[36] The City of Memphis also achieved sig-

nificant growth during the post-depression years. According to estimates, the population of Memphis grew from 253,143 inhabitants in 1930 to 292,942 in 1940, a 15.7% increase.[37]

In order to meet the increased banking demands of a growing city, Union Planters extended its branch banking operations by opening a Millington branch and a Cleveland Street branch in 1940-41. On the opening date of the Cleveland Street branch, June 30, 1941, "the Union Planters National Bank & Trust Company's Statement of Condition reflected total resources of $103,208,000, a gain of $16,274,000 over the total one year earlier. This gave the bank the distinction of being the only institution in the area, and one of 97 American banks, with resources over $100,000,000."[38]

Union Planters continued to grow during World War II. Its war effort, as described in the firm's financial statements for those years, included extending a large volume of loans to industries producing war goods and establishing a number of new services and facilities: a War Bonds sales department, a Ration Banking department, a depository and financial agency relationship with the U.S. Government, and a banking facility at the Kennedy General Hospital to serve war casualties and military personnel staff.[39]

In his January 9, 1946, report to the stockholders, Alexander stated his postwar strategy: "Our postwar plans not only include an aggressive program of seeking sound term loans to industry, commercial, agricultural and personal loans, but also a separate department for financing installment purchases of consumers' durable goods on a national scale."[40] As of the end of 1945, Union Planters reported total deposits of $221,921,027 and total resources of $234,936,493.[41] Thus the total resources of the bank had increased approximately

$134,000,000 during the 1941-45 war years, and Union Planters was in an excellent position to expand its operations. The post-war years were growth years for both Memphis and Union Planters. U.S. Census Bureau statistics show that Memphis experienced a 35.2% increase in population during the 1940-50 decade (from 292,942 to 396,000 inhabitants), and became the 26th largest city in the Nation.[42] Meanwhile, Union Planters continued its aggressive expansion program to meet the needs of the sprawling city.

During 1952, two noteworthy changes were made at Union Planters. On January 14, Alexander received permission from the acting Comptroller of the Currency to shorten the name of the bank from Union Planters National Bank & Trust Company to Union Planters National Bank of Memphis.[43] Then on April 10, 1952, the board of directors "elevated Mr. Alexander to chairman of the board and chief executive officer and elected Mr. [Arthur W.] McCain to succeed him as president. Mr. McCain, an Arkansan who began his banking career at Jonesboro, resigned as vice chairman of the board of the Chase National Bank of New York—world's third largest bank—to accept the local position."[44]

When McCain came to Union Planters as president, he found a rapidly expanding bank. By the end of 1952, Union Planters enjoyed an enlarged and remodeled main office, 11 branch banking facilities in Memphis, and an improved capital structure resulting from the successful sale of an additional 100,000 shares of common stock at $32 per share. Deposits had continued to climb and totaled $281,461,919, while total resources had grown to $311,956,381. Net profits after taxes for 1952 were $1,825,955, reflecting a 9.49% yield on capital funds.[45] McCain served as president of the bank for two years. On January 13, 1955, the Board of Directors promoted him to vice-chairman of the board, and John

E. Brown, executive vice president of Union Planters, succeeded McCain as president.

John Brown began his banking career in 1920 as a bookkeeper for the First State Bank in Henderson, Tennessee, his hometown. He worked diligently and advanced to that bank's presidency in 1937, a position he was to occupy for more than 20 years. While retaining that position, Brown joined Union Planters briefly in 1944 as assistant vice-president of the correspondent bank department, then moved to Jackson, Tennessee, in 1946 to become executive vice-president of the National Bank of Commerce; he returned to Union Planters in 1948 as manager of the correspondent bank department. Union Planters' management rehired him because of his extremely good relationship with the people in small neighboring communities who ran its correspondent banks.[46] Brown continued to serve as president of the First State Bank at Henderson, Tennessee, throughout his career at Union Planters. Brown's correspondent banking friends were elated when he became president of Union Planters. According to one newspaper account:

> John E. Brown, new president of Union Planters National Bank, was getting so many calls from his country banking friends today that the hundreds of Memphis business leaders trying to congratulate him could hardly get a word in.
>
> It was, "Hi, there John—you old farm boy! Congratulations."
>
> "Now listen, here Bill!" John said into a telephone, "you are talking to the president of the bank—wait until I switch you to a vice-president."
>
> Loud noises from the receiver. "You cotton-picking so and so, I've been president of a bank for years and you're already getting a swell-head!"[47]

As Union Planters entered the post-Korean War era, its leadership consisted of three men: Chairman of the

Board was Vance Alexander, the banking dynamo who had been 50 years old when he came to Union Planters as its president in 1933; who had brought the bank through the depression and the war years into its current prominence, but who was now 72 years old and in poor health; the Vice Chairman of the Board was Arthur McCain, a sophisticated former New York banker who had lived in Memphis for approximately 24 months; and the newly elected President was John Brown, a 53-year-old country banker who was acceptable to the Memphis business community, but whose greatest forte appeared to be his outstanding relationship with Union Planters' correspondent bankers and other country bankers.

Union Planters National Bank of Memphis continued to grow. In 1960 it announced that total resources had reached a record level of $428,258,924 as of December 31, 1960. During 1960, Union Planters' resources increased by $26,781,806; deposits increased by $15,856,566 to $380,690,815; and average daily loan volume rose by $7,718,000 to $193,464,000. Total loans outstanding at the end of 1960 were $206,819,518, an increase of $9,547,214. Net profits after taxes rose to $3,911,911 ($4.35 per share), compared with $3,271,215 ($3.63 per share) in the previous year. Total capital funds were $32,114,572.[48] Management accounted for these accomplishments in the following manner:

> This favorable accomplishment continues the trend of growth of your bank, and maintains for it the position as the largest bank in the entire Mid-South as well as a high place among the major banks of the nation.
> Our growth is in part a measurement of the over-all progress of the Mid-South . . . . Our business relations with other banks in the Mid-South area during 1960 was gratifying. More than 400 banks maintained active correspondent relations at Union Planters. A measurement of our success in serving correspondent

banks was a national ranking of 44th among the
'largest Banker's Banks' at September 30, 1960 . . . .

We take great pride again, as in the past, in telling
you that More Memphians Bank At Union Planters
Than At Any Other Bank . . . .[49]

As of December 31, 1960, Union Planters National
Bank of Memphis was "riding high"—the largest bank in
the Mid-South and, at the same time, earning record-
level profits.

3
BRANCH MANIA

The decade of the 1960s was a time of prosperity for the general economy of the United States. Spurred by the catalytic effect of the needs, wants, and demands of post-World War II babies reaching adulthood, the decade was economically volatile. At first, credit was relatively easy to obtain, but then became more difficult to find; and the cost of money changed from cheap to very, expensive. Construction of apartments, condominiums, second homes, and retirement facilities, as the nation prepared itself for the much-advertised leisure boom, expanded throughout the United States, particularly in the Southeast, Southwest, and West.

Construction of first-homes, entire neighborhoods in the suburbs, and accompanying shopping centers and office complexes to serve these newly developed neighborhoods also increased. Congress attempted to shape "the Great Society," distinguished by the elimination of all social ills. The "business world" attempted to respond to these Congressional goals by trying to define its social responsibilities. Experienced top management became unduly impressed with the wisdom of recent college graduates—the "young turks"—who were beginning to enter the job market. For expanding business concerns, real estate developers, would-be entrepreneurs and their bankers, this period can best be described as a "go-go" era.

In 1960 Union Planters had 18 banking offices, representing the culmination of 91 years of work and effort since the founding of the firm in 1869. During the 1960-

66 period, management implemented the greatest expansion program in the history of the bank and increased the number of its banking offices from 18 to 31. Stated another way, Union Planters was already the largest banking institution in the entire Mid-South at the opening of the 1960 decade, but increased its banking facilities by 72.2 percent during this six-year span. What factors brought about the need for this tremendous increase in facilities? What immediate and future effects did this increase in banking offices have on the firm's profitability?

During the 1950s, the population of the City of Memphis increased 25.6 percent, from 396,000 to 497,000 inhabitants. The Memphis Metropolitan Area (which includes Memphis and Shelby County) increased from 480,173 persons in 1950 to 627,019 in 1960, an increase of 30.5 percent.[50] Thus Memphis was continuing its steady growth. The economic climate of the city was favorable. Emphasis was being placed on the young generation, and competition between financial institutions to increase their respective market share was readily apparent. The greatest competitive struggle between local banking firms during the decade was the attempt of First National Bank and Union Planters, the city's two largest banks, to best each other in achieving an increased market share and in appearing to be the city's most aggressive, modern, growing financial institution.

Union Planters' expansion strategy was not a formal, written marketing plan designed to increase profits through better utilization of existing resources in order to fulfill changing, local banking needs. Rather, at times, it was simply management's response to the activities of First National Bank or of other local financial institutions. On January 11, 1961, Union Planters management announced an aggressive expansion program in its annual letter to stockholders:

Much attention has been given during the past year to meet the growing needs for banking facilities in Memphis. Our fine, new Manhattan Branch building at Madison and Second will be ready for occupancy early next month. Two additional offices scheduled for opening early in the year are the Galloway Park Branch in the Poplar Plaza Shopping Center at Poplar and Highland and the Mid-City Branch at Cleveland and Union. With these additions, Union Planters will have 20 banking locations in Memphis.[51]

The Bank acquired a site in southeast Memphis for a new Colonial branch in 1961, and began investigating modern electronic data processing installations.

During 1961, the Bank initiated a two-step capital expansion program. The first was to increase Union Planters common stock from $9,200,000 to $10,000,000 by declaring an $800,000 stock dividend (80,000 shares at $10 par value) on November 8, 1961. This stock dividend (plus the earlier 2.22 percent stock dividend declared at the 1960 annual meeting) gave stockholders more than 10.9 percent in dividends during the twelve month period.[52] The second step in the two-step capital expansion program was to increase Union Planters capital stock to $11,000,000 by issuing 100,000 shares of new common stock at $40 per share. Stockholder approval was obtained at the 1961 annual meeting. The new stock offering was made and subscribed to on February 7, 1962. In addition, Union Planters modernized and enlarged the main office and secured a permit to establish a branch office in the lobby of the then-new Memphis airport terminal during 1962.[53]

On January 10, 1963, the board of directors announced the retirement of Alexander, naming him honorary chairman of the board. The president of Union Planters, John Brown, was designated both president and chairman of the board. In the various news articles regarding Alexander's retirement, one compliment was most appropriate:

> As president of Union Planters from 1933 until 1952, and chairman of the board from then until yesterday, Mr. Alec not only presided over the great growth and progress of that bank, but also came to be known throughout the banking world as one of the most astute men in the entire field of finance. It has been said of him that he can analyze a proposition as quickly and surely as any banker in the business.
>
> And it has often been said of him that, if his analysis makes it necessary for him to turn the proposition down, he can say 'No' in a way that combines firmness and finality with kindness and an implicit invitation to come back again with a better proposition.[54]

When Alexander had come to Union Planters as president on April 8, 1933, the bank's deposits had been $25,879,926 and its capital structure approximately $5,200,000. On December 31, 1962, Union Planters deposits were $443,439,198, and its capital structure was $39,895,709.[55] On becoming honorary chairman of the board, Mr. Alexander said, "I've made mistakes, but all in all I think I've done pretty well—I've tried anyway."[56] The Vance Alexander reign was over.

During 1963, Union Planters became the first mid-South bank to open a New York office. The bank also opened three family banking centers: Memphis Metropolitan Airport, Frayser, and Whitehaven-South; it received permits to open new branches on Summer Avenue and in the Southgate Shopping Center; it relocated the Mid-City branch to the Mid-City Building and the North Memphis branch to the 100 North Main Building upon its completion; and it acquired additional capital through the successful sale of 150,000 shares of Union Planters stock, which yielded $6,000,000. As of December 31, 1963, Union Planters had capital funds of

$47,808,308. In January of 1964, John Brown explained the reasons for the continuous expansion program in his letter to the stockholders:

> Of almost equal importance to this strengthening of the bank's capital resources is its continued emphasis on 'taking the bank to the people.' Your directors feel that in the area of 'retail' banking there is a great growth potential and this business can be increased only by offering the public the convenience of 'Family Banking Centers' in their neighborhoods.[57]

In 1964, Union Planters management continued the branch expansion program. The Summer Center and Southgate branches (on which permits were received in 1963) were placed in operation as Family Banking Centers "keeping pace with the development of communities and shopping centers in Memphis."[58] The bank had 26 banking offices in Memphis at the end of 1964, but announced additional expansion plans for 1965—the opening of branches at Bellevue and Saxon, at White Station Road and Park Avenue, and at Park Avenue and Getwell. Management also purchased a quarter block at Front and Madison, across the street from Union Planters' Main Office, for a parking garage and a drive-in branch facility to replace the existing Front Street drive-in branch.

In his letter in January of 1965 to stockholders, Brown also stated that the bank had experienced another growth year with increased deposits and earnings, but he cautioned that 1965 should be viewed with guarded optimism. This note of caution, the first expressed during the 1960s, stemmed from the fact that most of the increase in overall deposits during 1964 had been in the form of savings and time certificates. The growth in savings and time deposits was due to Federal Reserve action in late 1963 which increased to 4% the interest rate banks were permitted to pay on time deposits. In November of 1964 the Federal Reserve again increased the allowable rate on time deposits to 4½%. Tennessee law, however, prohibited payment of more than 4% interest on time deposits. Brown predicted that corporations and large investors might move their short-term funds to another state, thus reducing deposits at Union Planters. But he also predicted that such a decline would not reduce earnings significantly, for profit margins were narrow.[59]

During 1964, Union Planters' deposits increased approximately as much as the increase in its loan volume (19 percent over 1963 loan volume). The increased loan volume, however, was primarily due to increased commercial and real estate loans. During the year, management increased the bank's loanable funds by transferring $2,500,000 to the Surplus account, which increased the bank's Surplus to $30,000,000. As of December 31, 1964, Union Planters capital structure was $50,023,687, an increase of $2,215,378 over the previous year. Earnings for 1964 were $3.67 per share, as compared with $3.35 per share in 1963.[60]

During 1965, Union Planters opened the Bellevue and Eastgate branches. That management planned to continue with its branch expansion strategy and development of Family Banking Centers was made clear in Brown's report to the bank's stockholders on January 19, 1966: "We now have 28 offices and will open at least two additional ones in 1966. Thus, we continue to maintain our leadership in the 'retail' banking field by offering the public maximum convenience in neighborhood banking."[61] Management also continued an investment policy described as follows: "We continue to strive for an advantageous investment position by keeping a substantial portion of our investment account in short-term securities so that we can reinvest for higher return as opportunities are presented."[62]

Union Planters management made organizational

changes during 1965 to: (1) centralize accounts information; (2) improve communications between policy makers and persons performing operational procedures; and (3) establish a department to pursue industrial business. Internal organizational problems regarding both accounts information retrieval and policy-operational communications are invariably tell-tale signs of an expansion program that is too rapid. They are the type of problems that should be corrected before continuing expansion. *THESE ORGANIZATIONAL MOVES WERE THE FIRST PUBLISHED SYMPTOMS THAT UNION PLANTERS NATIONAL BANK COULD BE HAVING INTERNAL PROBLEMS.*

The changes were described in the bank's 1965 *Annual Report* to its stockholders:

> In a major move to centralize vital account information and provide for faster retrieval from files, the Credit Department was expanded during 1965 and given responsibility for maintenance of central information files and 'Authorizations and Resolutions' files.
>
> . . . A Remington Rand file system with automatic equipment is being installed. This involves transferral of all central information data to new cards which will add to the efficiency and speed of obtaining data.
>
> More than 40,000 inquiries of various types were handled by the Credit Department during 1965, an average of about 20 inquiries per hour for every working day of the year . . . .
>
> Moving forward on a broad front of industrial development activity, Union Planters in 1965 appointed James B. Thurston, vice-president, to coordinate this function and provide specialized assistance to the many bank people already involved in promoting Mid-South industrial growth.
>
> Marketing organization of Union Planters Bank was strengthened late in the year by appointment of a Marketing Director whose primary function will be to

coordinate the many activities which fall under this title, and to improve communications between those responsible for policy and operational procedures.[63]

The bank's net earnings after taxes were excellent in 1965. Union Planters earned $5,112,232 ($4.09 per share, or 11.52% more than the record $3.67 per share earned in 1964).[64] But problems still persisted: In addition to the *internal* organizational problems, *external* problems also existed. Unfavorable legal and economic conditions prevailed which reduced the bank's earning power: First, *Tennessee law prohibited banks in the state from paying more than 4% interest on time deposits.* When the Federal Reserve raised the permissible interest rate on time deposits to 4½%, Union Planters' management correctly predicted that when short-term time certificates of deposit matured, they would be transferred to out-of-state financial institutions offering higher interest rates.

In 1965, Union Planters' average deposits, other than time certificates, increased approximately 5.6 percent over the previous year, but total deposits declined $1,854,929 to $525,986,068. Because Union Planters could not legally raise its rates to meet out-of-state competition for time certificates of deposit, available operating funds from this source of capital would continue to be reduced.[65]

Second, *The cost of money increased to Union Planters during the year.* With the prevailing increase in demand for loans, a tight money market occurred in 1965. In order to be competitive on savings deposits, on July 1, 1965, Union Planters raised its annual interest rate on passbook savings from 3½% to 4%, and also began to compound interest quarterly.[66] This adversely affected the gross earnings of the bank for six months in 1965. (The 4% interest rate and quarterly compounding of interest also would affect gross earnings throughout 1966.)

Brown's letter to stockholders in the 1965 Report stated, however, that the effects of the increased cost of savings deposits on gross earnings could be partially offset:

> On a more favorable side there was a 4.49% increase in average loan volume. Demand was strong throughout the year and activity was at a high level and is expected to continue so in 1966. Also favorable to future gross earnings is the recent increase by the Federal Reserve Board in the discount rate, which resulted in an increase in commercial loan rates. This should help offset the higher interest being paid on savings deposits.[67]

During 1965, average daily loan volume again reached an all-time high, $317,305,000.[68]

Thus, Union Planters National Bank was operating in a business climate characterized by: (1) inflation, (2) a "tight money" market, (3) the inability to favorably compete for time deposits, resulting in the probable reduction of capital as existing time deposits matured, (4) expansion programs by competing Memphis financial institutions, (5) continuing record loan volume, and, (6) record levels after tax earnings. The management of Union Planters must have concluded that the existing business strategy was proper.

The then-existing business strategy of Union Planters' management appears to have been: The answer to increased earnings is growth, growth, growth! Memphis is expanding, and Union Planters must take the bank to the people through branch expansion in order to remain the retail banking leader. Higher operating costs and interest expense on savings deposits would be offset by increased loan volume at higher interest rates. Meanwhile, the Bank would add to Surplus in order to increase loanable funds. The bank's capital structure would be protected by contributions from future earnings.

During 1966, C. Bennett Harrison was named president of the bank. John Brown retained his position as chairman of the board. Harrison had been with the First National Bank of Miami for 17 years before coming to Union Planters on March 1, 1965, as a vice president in the commercial loan division. Thus he had been with Union Planters for approximately one year before he became its president. In 1966, Union Planters had another record earnings year despite continued tight money conditions and high interest rates. Management continued its branch expansion strategy: three branches were opened during the year (Presidents Island drive-in branch, Holiday City branch, and South Perkins branch), and a branch at the White Station Tower was planned to open in 1967.

Total resources, average deposits, average loans, and net earnings after taxes achieved record levels. The changes that took place within these areas, however, give further insight into management's thinking and its then-present position. The total resources of the bank increased by $39,722,000 to $647,193,618. Cash due from other banks, investment volume, and fixtures resulting from branch expansion increased, but the significant change was in the tremendous increase in customers' liability acceptances. During the year, the bank increased its position in customer acceptances (representing both an asset and a liability to the bank), from $216,032 to $7,464,880, in an effort to increase future earnings.[69]

In 1965, management had increased overhead by adding two more branch operations while average deposits declined from $501,604,000 to $481,058,000. Management added three more branches in 1966 while average deposits climbed back to $501,434,000.[70] Thus *Union Planters, in 1966, had approximately the same number of average deposits as in 1964, but it also had the overhead expenses of five additional branch banking operations.*

Average loans increased during the year by $23,604,000 (7.4%) to $340,909,000.[71] This loan balance was achieved despite the fact that:

> The tight money market that prevailed in 1965 continued into 1966, making real estate financing extremely difficult, particularly in the latter part of the year . . . .
>
> At year-end demand for real estate financing continued to exceed the supply of money available. Lending institutions normally in the real estate field had curtailed their lending operations, and as a result there was a slowing down of real estate sales and construction. As demand continues high this activity should resume at an accelerated pace when money is more readily available.[72]

Management further stated that during 1966 "a number of personnel changes and additions were made to handle the increased volume of business and strengthen various departments. Several departments moved into new, larger quarters within the main banking office."[73] The above actions resulted in a 6.5% increase in the number of employees, from 983 to 1047.[74]

Brown and Harrison stated in their January 18, 1967, letter to the bank's stockholders:

> The year 1966 was a highly satisfactory one for your bank, with net operating earnings at a new record and all-time year-end highs established for loans, deposits and total resources.
>
> Net operating earnings for the year amounted to $5,510,846, or $4.41 per share. This compares with earnings of $5,112,232, or $4.09 per share, in 1965 . . .
>
> While the Mid-South's economic growth has been strong and we have confidence that it should continue healthy, we cannot overlook the fact that 1967 is clouded with uncertainties and should be approached with prudent caution . . . .[75]

In 1967, the White Station Tower branch opened and the DeSoto branch moved to a new location. The Kennedy Veterans Hospital facility was closed because of a "directive prohibiting any commercial business from being quartered in such institutions."[76] The net effect was that Union Planters was operating 31 banking facilities. For the first time since 1960, Union Planters management did not announce the opening of any additional banking facilities. *Implementation of the "branch expansion" strategy had ended.* Management was now pursuing new accounts through the introduction of the "bancardchek," card that was similar to a Traveler's Check and capable of being used anywhere[77]—the tentative beginnings of credit card banking.

Average deposits during 1967 increased by $37,405,000 to $538,839,000 (7.4%) and average loans outstanding increased by $7,161,000 to $348,070,000 (2.1%). Net operating earnings after taxes were $5,810,834 ($4.65 per share), compared with $5,510,846 ($4.41 per share) in 1966. Total capital funds increased by approximately $3.0 million to $58,522,481.[78]

At the August, 1967, board of directors meeting, Brown requested his retirement. In announcing the reasons for his retirement to newspaper reporters, he stated, "We have the bank well staffed with younger people. . . . It's time to turn it over to them. I'd like to do a little traveling. I've been a banker 47 years and seven months, and I've been too busy to do some of the things I'd like. I'm in good health, and I'd like to travel a bit while I can still enjoy it."[79]

On December 31, 1967, John Brown retired as chairman of the board. He was succeeded by C. Bennett Harrison. W. Porter Grace, executive vice president of the bank, succeeded Harrison as president of the Bank. The John Brown era at Union Planters was over.

4
GROPING FOR EARNINGS AND ORGANIZATION

When Ben Harrison became chairman of the board and chief executive officer of Union Planters on January 1, 1968, he assumed leadership of and responsibility for a banking institution with total resources of $709,174,816. Furthermore, the 1967 calendar year operations had resulted in record net earnings, with year-end deposits and loans at all-time highs. In their letter to the bank's stockholders regarding these 1967 earnings, Brown and Harrison noted unsettled economic conditions and credited the record earnings to "careful management of our assets."[80] About prevailing economic conditions, they commented:

Operating results were highly satisfactory in spite of an unsettled economic climate. Loan rates fluctuated during the year as well as the demand for money. Through careful management of our assets, however, we were able to maintain the flexibility necessary to meet these changing conditions.

We expect in 1968 a continuation of the characteristics of the economy that were experienced in the year just ended. Consumer demand for retail goods and services should remain strong. Credit costs can be expected to rise further and the serious problem of inflation will have an unsettling effect on our entire economy.

In our own local area we should see an increase in personal income and employment, particularly in manufacturing activities.[81]

Harrison was interviewed by a newspaper reporter concerning his thoughts regarding his new responsibilities for the direction and objectives of the bank, and the financial institution's future. In the interview, Harrison stated:

> Both here and nationally, UP has enjoyed an excellent reputation as an aggressive and innovative bank, and we are determined to continue to live up to that reputation. We are not a stand-still bank.
>
> We are going to find new and better ways of serving our customers, and we will grow and profit with them as this entire section of the country grows.
>
> I'm tremendously excited about what has been happening in the Mid-South. In place of what used to be an agrarian economy, we now have a very good balance of different types of commerce and industry. And it hasn't been all in one town or city. It has been all over, giving the entire region a solid base.
>
> This type of growth offers almost limitless opportunities for the banking business.[82]

Stating that he would rely heavily on modern marketing techniques in guiding Union Planters future course, Mr. Harrison said:

> I can't sit here at this moment and tell you exactly what innovations are going to be made, but I can say very definitely the marketing is going to help us pinpoint them.
>
> Our marketing department will play an important role in locating and defining those market segments and areas where we can be more effective. The research surveys have been with us for a number of years but, with the coming of the computer, the techniques of handling information have made the data much more accurate. We can now evaluate the data much more clearly.[83]

Regarding Union Planters future operations, Harrison predicted:

> [A]s this area grows, I think there is going to be a tremendous potential in the trust part of the banking business. At some point in the future, I foresee that our trust department is going to be a major part of the Union Planters set-up.
>
> I also think there is a credit card in our future. The credit card is not just a fad that will go away. It is becoming a normal part of banking. When some of the problems get straightened out there is going to be something like a truly universal credit card. When that happens, we'll be in on it.
>
> Meanwhile, we're well pleased with the acceptance of our Bancardchek guaranteed check, with its automatic overdraft feature.
>
> Despite the role to be played by computers, marketing surveys and credit cards, people will remain the single most important factor at UP.
>
> There is a wealth of talent here, and we have a continuing job to make it possible for them to do their best work. We have to find ways for them to grow with the bank, to upgrade them, because there is something new happening in banking all the time.[84]

During his first year as chairman, Harrison began to implement his management philosophy in three areas. The Bank: (1) established a separate Personnel Department, (2) completed development of the $3 million annex across from the Main Office, and (3) added two services to be offered to Union Planters' customers. In order to compete favorably for human resources in the banking industry, a bank must have modern recruitment, training and remuneration programs. In establishing a Personnel Department, Harrison employed a trained and experienced personnel manager to head the department. The compensation system was revised to meet the prevailing wage structure in the banking industry and in Memphis. Several surveys were conducted covering Memphis and the banking industry, and policies and procedures affecting personnel were modernized. An employee service recognition program was implemented. The Personnel Department also was charged with developing an extensive recruitment program at college campuses. Harrison was trying to develop an area in the Bank that he must have felt did not have sufficient emphasis under the former chairman.

Other innovations were implemented. To obtain new business, a successful sales incentive campaign was conducted. To improve communications among employees regarding activities within the various departments of the bank, an employee publication entitled "Bank Notes" was established within the Marketing Department. The $3 million annex under construction was expected to be completed in late 1969 or early 1970. Its purpose was to provide parking facilities, a drive-in banking facility, and facilities for the operations department of the bank.[85]

Although the bank appeared to have ended its "branch expansion" strategy, existing branches were being upgraded and remodeled. During 1968, the Raleigh branch was remodeled and drive-in windows were added. Drive-in windows and parking facilities were also added to the Mid-City branch in 1968. The Madison Avenue branch was expected to move from its temporary quarters into a new office building in the medical center in 1969. The Whitehaven-South branch also would be moving from its leased space into new branch facilities in 1969. Two new services were added by Union Planters. The bank entered the credit card business by joining the Master Charge group in the Fall of 1968. In November, personal checking account service charges were changed from a sliding scale to a flat fee of $1.50 for account balances under $500, regardless of the number of checks written.[86]

The 1968 year-end figures showed net operating earnings after taxes of $5,187,706, compared with $5,810,834 for 1967. Adjusted for a 20% stock dividend declared during the year, 1968 per share earnings fell 41 cents, from $3.87 to $3.46. Operating income during 1968 increased by $4,105,134 to $34,080,052; however, total operating expenses increased by $4,207,712, to $26,043,828. With the incorporation of the new remuneration system and the addition of 98 employees (a 9.0% increase in the bank's staff), salaries increased by $851,429. Pensions, profit sharing, and other employee benefit expenses increased by $272,022 to $987,608. Other increases in the bank's operating expenses stemmed from new program offerings and the higher cost of doing business.[87]

Because of Tennessee's ceiling on interest rates, the bank was faced both with high overhead expenses and the increasing cost of funds because of a tight money market, but could not recoup some of these costs through raising interest rates. Although management had stopped its branch expansion strategy, management, judging by its actions, must have felt that it needed to continue its development of a modern bank image. Total resources of the bank increased to $724,918,890 in 1968, an all-time high. However, an analysis of the resources reveals that the structure of those resources was changing. Cash and amounts due from other banks declined during the year by more than $6,000,000. Management increased its investments in U.S. Government obligations by more than $26,000,000. Loans increased by $8,300,000 to $391,903,903 as of December 31, 1968. Average loans for the year were $370,079,000, a $22,009,000 increase over the previous year. Customer acceptance liabilities were reduced by $5,594,205 to $721,403.[88]

Thus, following his first year as chairman of the board, Harrison was confronted with the following conditions as the 1969 business year began: (1) an inflationary economy, in which the costs of conducting normal banking operations were increasing; (2) a tight money market, in which the cost of money (the commodity purchased and/or sold by a bank in order to pay overhead costs and hopefully generate profits) was increasing; (3) narrowing gross profit margins on loans, resulting from the bank's inability to pass on to the borrower increasing costs of funds (due to Tennessee's ceiling on interest rates); (4) continued demands on capital for branch remodeling and other programs, designed to give the bank an aggressive, modern banking image and improve its market share of deposits; (5) continued pressure on earnings because of management's apparent decision to maintain a dividend policy requiring $2,400,000 annually (46.26% of the bank's 1968 earnings) in order to keep existing stockholders satisfied and attract new stockholders; and (6) continued internal problems, causing management to attempt to implement: (a) an internal communications program to inform existing employees of the bank's strategies, policies, and procedures; and (b) a management training program to motivate and train existing employees, enhance the image of a modern bank, and attract new employees to the firm.

Together, prevailing economic conditions, legal restrictions, and management-formulated and -implemented programs and policies had produced a banking firm with declining earnings margins as well as some loss in liquidity.

During 1969, Union Planters continued to implement Harrison's strategy. It was the year of the Bank's 100th birthday. Except for the day when President

Roosevelt gave all banking institutions a holiday, Union Planters had been open every business day since September 1, 1869. A large number of public relations activities were conducted to celebrate the event. Throughout the anniversary year numerous comments were made regarding existing banking conditions and the future of banking. Harrison revealed his thoughts about banking's future in an article published in *Mid-Continent Banker*:

> The fact that Union Planters has been in existence 100 years and that thousands of Memphians refer to UP as 'my bank' has not intoxicated present management. The management team at Union Planters is looking not at the past but to the future.
>
> This is an exciting time for banking and the future will be even more so. Banks, in my opinion, will venture more and more into related fields either through the holding company route or by liberalization of current regulatory restrictions. Certainly, banks will step-up their customer-oriented services in the area of credit cards, guaranteed checks and pre-authorization of payment of such consumer charges as utility bills, telephone bills and similar items.[89]

Thomas A. Garrison, vice president of Branch Administration, echoed Harrison's thoughts regarding branch banking, in an article published by the *Daily News*:

> According to T. A. Garrison, the nation's banks had less than a dozen branches in 1890. Today, Union Planters alone has 30 branches in the Memphis area.
>
> A bank branch is important not only to individuals living in the vicinity of the facility, but to nearby local business firms and to national corporations which have regional offices in Memphis. All of the varied publics that are located throughout Greater Memphis find branch banking far more convenient than coming into the downtown area to complete their banking transactions.

A customer, whether an individual or a business firm, can obtain every service at a bank branch that he can at Union Planters' three major banking houses in the downtown area.

Mr. Garrison pointed out that it wasn't until 1925 that laws began to be passed governing branch banking. It was that same year that Tennessee enacted a statute limiting the establishment of branches to the same county in which the main office of the bank was located.[90]

In October 1969, Union Planters made a top management organization move. Porter Grace ascended from the presidency to vice chairman of the board, and James C. Merkle, 42, president of the First National Bank of Anniston, Alabama, became president. "In three years there (First National Bank, Anniston, Alabama), earnings went from $400,000 to $700,000. Assets of the bank during his term as president increased from 43 million dollars to 57.8 million."[91] The announcement that Merkle had become president brought considerable publicity to Union Planters. *Finance* magazine wrote:

> On the eve of its 100th anniversary, Union Planters Bank, Memphis, Tennessee, is accenting "youth" . . . ."Appointing Merkle represented a conscious attempt to get some new young blood into the Union Planters organization," the bank says . . . .
>
> By 1970, Union Planters expects to complete construction of a nine-story annex across from its main office. The focus is on expansion of facilities and business, as Union Planters enters its second 100 years.[92]

And the *American Banker* stated: "His [Merkle's] appointment marks the second time in recent years that a president has been named from outside the bank."[93]

In describing the results of the bank's operations in 1969, Harrison, Grace, and Merkle took the opportunity

James C. Merkle, President. Union Planters National Bank, 1969-1973.

to comment on current economic conditions and the position of banking institutions:

As Union Planters begins its second century of service, it does so at a time of inflation, tight money, high interest rates, and other economic problems. While banks did not create the monetary clampdown on the nation's economy, they did become the victims of the public's thinking as interest rates zoomed and consumer prices spiraled even higher.

When inflation is brought under control, we believe the outlook will be much brighter than it was as 1969 came to a close. For it is a certainty that banks profit best when business growth continues at a stable pace.

The effect of current restrictive monetary policies has been severe on the entire banking industry. We are hopeful this period precedes one in which Union Planters will again enjoy higher earnings and continue its objective of growth and achievement in all areas of the bank.[94]

Analysis of the operations of Union Planters in 1969 shows that after tax net operating earnings rose to $5,046,915 (a 3.5% increase over 1968 earnings), and operating income increased (by 16.4%) to $39,697,428, primarily because of increases in interest and fees on loans and in income from securities. Total deposits remained approximately the same as in 1968 ($638,000,000), but average loan balances increased by more than $12,000,000. However, total loans at year end had decreased by more than $8,000,000. Operating expenses were $31,701,563 ($4,998,226, or 18.7%, higher than 1968 operating expenses). Interest costs accounted for over 48% of total operating expenses. Employee salaries and benefits increased by more than $1,500,000 to exceed $8,000,000, and accounted for 21.43% of operating expenses.[95]

Management explained to its stockholders the necessity for the higher salaries and benefits:

> Expansion of customer services and an increase in the volume of activity in several departments made staff additions mandatory during the year. It was desirable, too, to adjust salary scales upward to retain qualified personnel and to attract competent new employees, especially on the managerial level.[96]

During the year, management hired 85 additional employees (a 6.8% increase), bringing the total number of Union Planters employees to 1,322 persons.[97] (In 1966, 31 banking facilities had been operated by 177 fewer persons.) During 1969, management again paid $2,400,000 to its stockholders ($1.60 per share), continuing the dividend policy of previous years. This outlay represented 52.7% of the bank's net income in 1969. Total capital funds were $61,870,354.[98]

At the beginning of 1970, the prime rate of interest was at an unprecedented 8½%, but by the end of the year, it had fallen to 6¾%. The easing of tight money conditions was favorable to bankers and other businessmen, and was an important external economic factor providing management with an opportunity to increase earnings. At Union Planters, 1970 was a year in which management focused primarily on improving one major internal factor—better organization of the firm. When asked to designate the bank's most important achievement during 1970, Jim Merkle replied:

> I think there were really two. We created a Corporate Planning function which we believe will provide us with new opportunities that will be advantageous to the progress of the bank in the Seventies.
>
> By separating Corporate Planning from day-to-day line responsibilities, the long-range goals of the bank can be established much more objectively.
>
> Second, the board of directors of Union Planters and its affiliate, Manhattan Savings Bank and Trust Co., adopted resolutions whereby Union Planters would acquire all the assets of Manhattan Savings Bank in exchange for Union Planters stock.[99]

The Corporate Planning area, referred to by Merkle, was a new department created for the purpose of functioning in four specific areas: asset management, short and long range planning, management information systems, and financial analysis. The asset management function of the department was to control the bank's role as a financial intermediary. As the source of contact between parties with available funds and parties with a need for funds, Corporate Planning decided where the capital could best be obtained as well as where it could best be employed. The short range planning function consisted of developing a comprehensive annual profit plan for the bank. The long range planning function involved developing corporate goals (manpower, space, equipment needs), "an attempt to determine how to best make an orderly transition, from Union Planters as it exists today, to meet conditions that will confront commercial banking in the years ahead."[100]

The management information systems function consisted of developing the tools necessary to formulate the annual profit plan. Under this approach, managers evaluated opportunities and planned for the future. Utilizing a responsibility reporting system approach, each organizational unit within the bank received a monthly report of its income and expenses in order to better control costs and evaluate future performance. The financial analysis function included the development of special studies for management's consideration. These studies emphasized such things as improving profitability of services and the pricing of services.

The objectives of Corporate Planning for the next year (1971) were: (1) to implement an asset management system; (2) to enlarge the Management By Objectives approach to include additional units within Union Planters; (3) to develop a profit center reporting system, to identify and report all income and expense items by invididual profit centers; and (4) to expand financial analysis activities, with particular emphasis on the total account relationship with a customer, to assist management in studying the ever important profitability contributions of major accounts.[101]

During 1969, Union Planters also reorganized its Control Division. The objective was to centralize the general accounting and the control functions into a single department, and to improve internal management reporting by installing a responsibility reporting system. Some of these goals were accomplished, for, by the end of the first quarter of 1970, Union Planters was able to begin mailing quarterly reports of earnings to its stockholders. The primary objective for 1971 was to improve internal information reports to management.[102]

During 1970 the Personnel Department hired a training professional from the Bendix Corporation and developed, for the first time, a formalized program for indoctrination and orientation of new employees. The personnel department also conducted supervisory seminars, seminars for middle management, and an executive training program for top management. Another accomplishment was the increased use of part-time employees:

> The bank had about 1,290 full-time people at year-end. During 1970 we increased our efforts to utilize part-time employees in positions formerly occupied by full-time personnel. By so doing we made more effective use of manpower and at the same time had more efficient control over the overall personnel expense to the bank. For example, costs of overtime pay were reduced by 25 per cent compared to 1969.[103]

During 1970 the Investment Department reduced its U.S. government holdings and substantially increased its investment in state and municipal bonds, which produced both an increase in investment income and a reduction in Federal income tax for the year. The Investment Department also reduced the inventory in the bank's trading account by approximately $26,000,000. The Investment Department contributed $10,480,881 to Union Planters' Operating Income in 1970, 23% of the bank's total operating income for the year. During 1969, the Investment Department had contributed $7,762,442 to Union Planters' total operating income (19.6% of the $39,461,230 total operating income for that year).[104] The Investment Department also expanded its operations in 1970:

> Management was vitally interested in the growth of this department and we had to add a number of people to our staff in order to adequately handle the increased volume of business.
>
> We installed trading desks for U.S. Government issues, agencies of the Federal Government and municipal issues. These trading desks, staffed by trained personnel, enabled us to better serve correspondent banks, corporations and individuals.
>
> We also enlarged our merchandising operations by adding sales personnel who specialize in selling bonds to correspondent banks and individuals.[105]

Union Planters' net operating earnings after taxes during 1970 were $6,048,069, a 67 cents per share increase (to $4.03 per share, compared with $3.36 in 1969). When asked to what he attributed the 20% increase in earnings, Merkle replied: "It was primarily due to the change in our investment mix."[106] The total resources of Union Planters increased by $147,769,790 in 1970, from $730,002,200 to $877,771,990. Of that amount, cash and amounts due from banks totalled $186,758,376 (21.2%). Thus, loans during 1970 increased by $99,145,536 (a 26.2% increase) to $476,638,956, and accounted for 54.3% of the bank's total resources. During the same period, interest and fees on loans contributed

$30,059,282 to earnings, a $2,244,048 increase (8.0%) over the 1969 contribution, and accounted for 66.5% of Union Planters' total operating income. Total capital funds at year end were $63,025,993.[107]

Porter Grace, vice-chairman of the board of directors, retired on December 31, 1970. The position was not filled after his retirement.

5
DESIGN FOR THE FUTURE

In Union Planters' *1970 Annual Report*, Merkle had listed the primary objectives of the bank for 1971:

> Briefly, we want to make more effective use of our resources, we want to increase the efficiency of every division and department and we want to improve service to our customers. The year 1970 was one of planning and defining these objectives and 1971 will be the year they will be put into action.
>
> By the fall of 1971 the Operations Division will be housed in the new Annex being built across the street from the main banking office. This move will result in a tremendous advancement in efficiencies that will not be restricted to Operations alone but to numerous other areas of the bank, including all the branches.
>
> In 1971 also will be the year in which we are going to encourage people who are doing their banking elsewhere to step UP to Union Planters.[108]

In an article entitled "Bankers Expect Growth Despite Economic Conditions," which appeared in *The Memphis Press Scimitar* early in 1971, Merkle said he was "highly optimistic about the future of both the city and the bank," and that he was "enthusiastic about plans for new equipment and programs to update every department of the bank."[109] He pointed out:

> Madison will house expanded computer operations, data processing center, an enlarged transit department, five levels of parking and a rooftop heliport.
>
> Two new branches in the planning stages will bring

the total number to 33, and other locations in the growing suburbs are under consideration.

The new Computa-Home program will be promoted. This computerized house-hunting service offers free to newcomers a description of 20 homes which most nearly match the applicant's specifications.

A new payroll-deposit plan will use a computer to handle small businesses and payrolls, avoiding the time spent standing in line on payday to cash or deposit salary checks.

Construction of new buildings interests the bank, which is now financing the new Clark Tower in East Memphis.[110]

Merkle also predicted that, "[a]s a growing city, unhampered by the massive labor problems besetting some metropolitan areas, Memphis should continue to progress in a healthy business and industrial climate."[111]

While Merkle was projecting continued expansion and good times for the bank, Harrison was commenting on some of the many problems which the bank faced:

Of the many problems facing bankers as 1971 gets underway, I would like to comment on three I consider most important.

Inflation continues to be one of the most persistent problems and must be faced again this year. Political pressures have forced a change in governmental policy to combat inflation, but it remains to be seen how effectively the Administration can deal with this problem through renewed emphasis on wage and price guidelines . . . .

A second problem faced by bankers will be increased competition from within the industry as well as from other types of financial institutions.

Many one-bank holding companies have been formed to adequately meet this competition through diversification. This is a healthy development for the banking industry because with increased competition will come improved efficiencies, a broader range of services and better quality of services for financial customers.

Commercial paper, I believe, will continue to be a major competitor of banks for the short term financing of our business customers. Non-bank-related commercial paper reached the $30-billion level last year, which is equivalent to 37½% of bank commercial loans.

The need for improving profitability will be a third problem facing bankers this year. Inflationary and competitive pressures make this an even greater challenge . . . .We need to do a better job of planning for both short and long range needs.

Our managers and employees are our most important asset . . . .A comprehensive training program continues to be emphasized at our bank, and many other banks will be taking similar steps this year.[112]

The business climate of 1971 indeed was different from that of 1970. In 1970, tight money conditions had prevailed, and many banks had not been in a position to meet loan demand. In 1971, however, more lendable funds became available because businessmen deferred expansion and consumers increased their savings. Prime interest rate competition was keen among Memphis banks. In January of 1971, the prime rate was 6¾%. By December of 1971, Union Planters' prime interest rate was 5¼%.

In reporting the 1971 operating results, Harrison and Merkle announced that "total assets at year-end, for the first time in the 102-year history of your bank, exceeded one billion dollars."[113] Of the $1,048,719,824 in assets held by Union Planters on December 31, 1971, loans accounted for $517,585,660 (49.3%). Investment securities, which increased $54,988,167 (30.7%) during the 12-month period, totaled $233,662,153 (22.3% of the bank's assets). Cash and amounts due from other banks were $196,230,767 (18.7% of total assets).[114] Average deposit balances increased by $136,684,000 (22.7%), from $600,449,000 in 1970 to $737,133,000 in 1971. Average demand deposit balances climbed $37,061,000 to $348,258,000, compared with $311,197,000 in 1970. Average time deposit balances increased by $99,623,000 (34.4%) to $388,875,000.[115] However, operating earnings before taxes and securities gains and losses decreased by $1,374,425 to $7,248,598. While operating income increased from $45,911,164 to $51,411,916 (an 11.9% increase) during 1971, operating expenses increased even faster, from $37,288,141 to $44,163,318 (an 18.4% increase).[116]

From the time he had assumed office as chairman of the board four years before and became responsible for leading the bank to achieve its objectives, Harrison must have had some very soul-searching moments. During Alexander's reign as president and chairman of the board, the bank had achieved record growth as well as record earnings. The pattern of record growth and earnings continued under his successor, John Brown. When Harrison succeeded Brown, his actions demonstrated his recognition that the bank lacked both organization and trained executive leadership at the middle and upper managerial echelons. Merkle, as president, was responsible for the daily operations of the institution and for organizing the bank to operate efficiently.

During 1970 Union Planters' management had created a Corporate Planning function to plan and define the bank's objectives for 1971, "the year they will be put into action."[117] The *1970 Annual Report* described the structure of Union Planters as composed of: Operations Division, Commodity Loans and International Services area, Correspondent Bank Department, Commercial Loans Department, Real Estate Loans area, Personnel Division, Investment Department, Trust Department, Marketing Division, Control Division, Metropolitan Division, Installment Credit area, Corporate Planning, and National Accounts. The bank also had an affiliate, Manhattan Savings Bank and Trust Company, which, pending stockholder approval, the board had voted to absorb into the bank.[118]

During 1971 the shareholders approved the Manhattan transaction. Union Planters acquired all of the assets of its affiliate, Manhattan Savings Bank and Trust Company, the stock of which had been held in trust for the benefit of Union Planters stockholders. In exchange, "225,000 shares of Union Planters common stock were issued to Union Planters stockholders on the basis of one additional share for each five and two-thirds owned. Fractional shares were sold and the proceeds remitted in cash to the proper shareholders."[119] The bank also purchased the 100 North Main Building, completed the 10-story Annex, constructed one new branch, and remodeled three of its older branches during 1971.[120]

Management significantly changed the organizational structure of the bank during the year, describing the functions of the bank's various Divisions as follows:

> The largest, and certainly the area most familiar to customers of the bank, is the Retail Banking Division, which includes the entire Branch System, Business Development, Sales Training, and two previously separate departments, Installment Credit and Master Charge.
>
> . . . [The Automation Division] was formed in 1971 following separation of the automation functions from the Operations Division.
>
> By combining National Accounts and Correspondent Banks into a newly established Corporate Division, Union Planters was able to considerably strengthen all of its activities outside the metropolitan Memphis area but within the continental United States.
>
> The Trust Division . . . in the past three years alone,

... has grown from 46 to 68 employees and more than doubled its officer ranks.

The Investment Division will continue to participate in high-grade issues that will result in reasonable profits for your bank. Further expansion of the division's staff is planned for 1972 . . . .

Planning and Administration division, . . . established during 1971, was formed by linking existing staff functions into a single group. Corporate Planning, Control, Marketing, Audit, and Administrative Services all became a part of Planning and Administration, as did three newly created departments—Economics, Economic Development and Information Systems.

Perhaps the most significant area of change in the entire bank during 1971 occurred in the Loan Division . . . . Three existing departments [Real Estate, Commodity Loans, the Credit Department] and two new departments [Accounts Receivable Financing and Loan Services] were consolidated under the umbrella of Commercial Loans. The international banking function was separated from commodities activities and centralized in the International Finance Department . . . .

. . . [T]he Operations Division . . . , by systems, procedures and specialized equipment, controls the daily flow of paperwork through the bank.

. . . [T]he Personnel Division . . . transferred its entire officer and staff information records to a computer, becoming one of the first banks in the country . . . to do so.[121]

During 1971, Union Planters also embarked on two new courses of action which would prove to be of substantial significance in the coming years. One innovation was the decision to become a bank holding company. The second was to retain an outside accounting firm to provide financial reporting and management consulting services to the bank.

During Union Planters 100th birthday celebration in 1969, Harrison had expressed an appreciation of the bank holding company concept as a way to expand into related fields.[122] For example, a holding company, which is regulated by the Federal Reserve, could operate banking offices throughout Tennessee, whereas a national bank, which is regulated by the Comptroller of the Currency, could not. In October of 1971, management was authorized by the board of directors to:

> proceed with the organization of a bank holding company to be known as Union Planters Corporation. Under the proposed plan, the bank would become a wholly-owned subsidiary of the holding company. Present bank directors and executive management would retain their same capacities.
>
> The new corporate structure, if approved by the shareholders and various governmental agencies, will be effective May 1, 1972. Union Planters National Bank will carry on its original banking business under its current bank name.[123]

Unlike national banks, which are chartered by the federal government, bank holding companies are chartered under state law. As such, they are subject to the rules and regulations of the Securities Exchange Commission, including financial reporting requirements. Financial statements must be prepared in accordance with Generally Accepted Accounting Principles, and must be examined and reported on by an independent accounting firm. A comparison of the 1971 and 1970 Annual Reports illustrates the difference this made for Union Planters.

While Harrison was pursuing holding company status, Merkle was seeking ways to strengthen the bank's internal audit and control capability. Earlier in the Harrison-Merkle era, the bank had retained Peat, Marwick,

Mitchell & Co., one of the "big eight" accounting firms, as a consultant on special projects (e.g., to design a responsibility reporting system). Management also had been considering hiring an outside auditing firm to prepare the bank's financial statements, an innovation which would be expensive and was not required by law. In mid-1971, Merkle initiated discussions with several major public accounting firms to explore the bank's need for outside auditors and management consulting services, as well as the accounting firms' ability to meet those needs. In late 1971 those discussions culminated in the hiring of Peat, Marwick, Mitchell & Co. for 1971 and subsequent years.

Before that firm was hired, however, the SEC changed the rules governing bank holding company financial reports. Until late 1971, the SEC permitted independent auditors to report on a bank holding company's financial statements without examining any of its bank subsidiaries so long as the bank's internal auditor verified the figures in conformity with the requirements of bank regulatory authorities. Only the holding company itself (and any non-bank subsidiaries) had to undergo an independent audit. Thus, although becoming a one-bank holding company meant subjection to the SEC, that alone did not necessitate incurring the considerable expense of a complete external audit. However, late in 1971, the SEC stopped accepting holding company financial statements which relied on verified internal bank figures. Thus implementation of management's plan to form Union Planters Corporation during 1972 suddenly became dependent upon the bank itself obtaining a complete independent audit for 1971 and subsequent years. Thus a change in regulations by the SEC made consideration of the two separate innovations inseparable.

On November 1, 1971, Peat, Marwick, Mitchell & Co. addressed a letter to Harrison which set out in detail the firm's qualifications to perform the examination for Union Planters. The letter also described the approach that firm proposed to follow in carrying out the engagement, and included "other pertinent information."[124] The four-page letter stated, in part:

" . . . PMM & Co. is the recognized leader in bank accounting and auditing.

We feel that the examination of Union Planters National Bank can be accomplished most effectively by the "round-the-clock approach." Under this approach, we make an in-depth evaluation of effectiveness of operating procedures and controls through the observation of, and participation with, the Bank's own auditing department throughout the year, and the application of analytical auditing techniques.

. . . We would plan to submit a letter to management, at the conclusion of our examination, containing our observations, comments and suggestions concerning internal controls, operating and accounting procedures, and other matters worthy of management consideration.

Memphis office personnel have the necessary knowledge and experience to carry out the examination of Union Planters National Bank in efficient and competent manner. Nevertheless, recognizing the unique requirements of auditing one of the largest banks in the United States and considering your intended desire to form a registered bank holding company, we have made arrangements to obtain assistance [from a partner in St. Louis] who has extensive experience in auditing some of our largest banking clients and in assisting numerous banks form registered bank holding companies.

We continue to consult with Bank officers regarding . . . prior engagements [which] give us familiarity with the Bank's accounting system which will be of value to us . . . . [W]e will absorb first year start-up costs . . . . [M]utually satisfactory fee arrangements can be made at a level commensurate with the services to be rendered. We . . . have arranged to commit the necessary resources to this engagement to assure you of the highest quality of performance."[125]

Attached to the letter was a 14-page proposal which set out in additional detail the expertise and services which the bank would obtain from Peat, Marwick, Mitchell & Company. In summary, the expertise was described as follows: the proposal noted that Peat, Marwick, Mitchell & Company had specialized for decades in auditing and management consulting services for banks, depicted the firm's extensive banking practice and expertise, particularly in connection with the formation and operation of bank holding companies, described the experienced personnel who would be assigned to work with Union Planters, and stated that these services "would be performed throughout the year and would include involvement in all major operating departments of the bank."[126]

The actual services which would be provided also were described: (1) "Overall Review and Evaluation of Operating Procedures and Controls"; (2) "determine the degree of adherence to the prescribed operating procedures of the Bank, and thus assess the functioning of the system of internal control;" (3) "ongoing analytical review of financial statements, account balances and transactions in order to detect situations requiring investigation;" (4) "evaluating the overall quality of the loan portfolio[,] adequacy of the related reserve for loan losses[, and] overall lending policies and practices;" and (5) "innovative suggestions for improvements (if any) in [existing] controls."[127] The services were described as a "round-the-clock" audit approach to the bank's needs.[128] The proposal noted that the complete "round-the-clock" approach could not be used for 1971 (which was almost over), but it did state that the 1971 examination would include:

"[R]eview [of] the system of internal control, including the effectiveness of the internal audit effort. . . . Verification of assets and liabilities . . . on a surprise basis . . . [E]valuation of loans on a test basis, review of administration of selected trust accounts, and verification of various asset and liability accounts. . . . [And] a letter to management containing our observations, comments and suggestions concerning internal control, operating and accounting procedures, and other matters worthy of management consideration."[129]

The proposal concluded with a listing of the broad range of additional benefits which Peat, Marwick, Mitchell & Company, as a "full service firm," would make available to the bank. It noted that, in addition to assistance on audit and tax matters, client benefits included consulting services which "cover a broad spectrum"; publications "covering timely matters of interest"; imaginative practical approaches to [S.E.C.] accounting and reporting problems, particularly as related to registering securities and reporting on mergers and acquisitions"; and seminars for Bank personnel on various topics.[130]

The Peat, Marwick, Mitchell & Co. proposal must have seemed ideal to Union Planters management. It promised to solve the two major problems facing the bank in 1972: getting Union Planters Corporation into operation, and establishing the first-rate internal control capability so necessary to further expansion as a billion dollar holding company.

Meanwhile, the general economy of the United States was characterized by inflation. The government took measures to slow down the economy which produced a tight money market and hampered the bank's earnings by increasing the cost of funds. In Tennessee this situation was aggravated by the interest ceiling which had been established by the legislature. The bank had to maintain a larger loan and deposit volume to carry its large overhead expenses. Yet the increasing cost of funds, coupled with Tennessee's ceiling on what a bank could charge for loans, seriously reduced profit margins and earnings. The same general economic conditions and outside pressures that were affecting Union Planters also affected other local banks. Keen competition resulted, particularly from the First National Bank of Memphis, which was also trying to maintain an aggressive, modern image through branch expansion and other programs.

During the late 1960s and early 1970s, the Memphis Chamber of Commerce had launched a campaign to develop a favorable image for Memphis by telling the Nation about "Mid-America's Big New City." Both Harrison and Merkle were active members of the Chamber, and Union Planters became heavily involved in the campaign. Had management wished to defer formation of the holding company, close branches, reduce payroll, or implement other cost-cutting measures, these actions would have conflicted with the Chamber's program and probably would have resulted in Union Planters losing its aggressive, modern image.

Because of a large increase in deposits due to businessmen's and consumer's conservatism while unfavorable economic conditions persisted, Union Planters became a "billion dollar" bank in 1971. Although loans increased, interest and fees on loans as a source of operating income increased only slightly (by less than $1,300,000) during 1970 because of borrower conservatism and lower interest rates. Yet management prepared to embark on the unfamiliar ground of operating a bank holding company—and also continued to invest heavily in expansion. Bank premises and equipment more than doubled from $14,762,779 in 1970 to $29,849,988 at the end of 1971. Fifty-nine more employees were added in 1971, increasing the number to 1,349, while salaries and wages increased by $1,028,484 (12.6%) to $9,166,881.[131] Management had also added the ongoing expense of "round-the-clock" audit and consulting services by independent auditors.

Because of general economic conditions, loan demand, and keen competition, the bank became ever more dependent upon assuming larger positions in investment securities as a means of improving operating income. In 1970, interest and dividends on investment securities constituted 15.1% of Union Planters' operating earnings. In 1971 the figure was 20.6%. Thus by investing more heavily in securities, management was able to obtain sufficient operating income to offset increased overhead expenses and to make a profit as well.[132] Thus Union Planters was a billion dollar bank attempting, with the assistance of "the recognized leader in bank accounting and auditing," to formulate and implement extensive organizational changes in an uncertain economic climate. The economy was inflationary, highly unpredictable, and extremely sensitive to any changes in federal policy—such as adopting stricter measures to fight inflation. The nature of resulting shifts in the attitudes of investors and consumers was equally uncertain. In this context the bank's management continued to implement a difficult strategy.

At the beginning of 1972, Memphis bankers felt bullish about the local economy despite President Nixon's installation of wage-price controls. Their reasoning:

> Memphis has the type of economic balance that neither booms nor busts and makes bankers smile.
>
> Bankers are quick to point out examples of diversification whenever discussing the mood of the Memphis economy. Manufacturing claims 20 per cent of the economic pie; government, 19 per cent; retail, 16 per cent; service, 16 per cent; and no other sector that makes up as much as 10 per cent.[133]

At the 10th annual economic development conference sponsored by Union Planters, the consensus of industrial leaders was: "The Mid-South area economy has enjoyed substantial gains in recent months, and all indicators point to continued growth."[134] This forecast was generally accepted, and bankers aggressively pursued business.

One way in which Memphis bankers chose to increase loan volume was to establish a prime rate based on local conditions. In early January of 1972, when the Bank of America (the largest bank in the United States) announced an immediate reduction in its prime interest rate from 5¼% to 5%. Memphis bankers did not follow. Harrison, in a newspaper interview explained:

> [R]egional banks about six months ago began establishing their best commercial lending rate on local conditions and the competitive factors of their region.
>
> This situation evolved as many of the money-center banks have been seeking a formula to tie the . . . prime . . . rate to other short-term yields of money market instruments. This has brought about, in a number of banks, what is called a floating prime rate, which might change weekly according to money market conditions.
>
> . . . It will take a while to see how it will work out.
>
> . . . Our consumer rate on personal loans is 6 per cent—the same as it was in 1927 when we opened our personal loan department.[135]

Based on additional interviews with several other Memphis bankers, the newspaper reporter reached the following conclusion:

> It boils down to being competitive. Can a Memphis business executive with the proper credentials privately negotiate a loan rate below a bank's publicly announced prime figure? Memphis bankers say each corporate loan application is judged on its own merits.[136]

During the first quarter of 1972, Union Planters bought some property near the 100 North Main Building, opened the Raleigh branch, emphasized trust services, and announced that shareholders had approved reorganizing the banking operation as a subsidiary of a new bank holding company, Union Planters Corporation. On April 10, 1972, prospects for the fledgling Union Planters Corporation were reviewed in *The Wall Street Transcript*. The article concluded:

> Marketing strength comes from long association with commodity and real estate-oriented operations as well as the correspondent banking group; the retail banking division; the trust department; and the bond underwriting division. Aggressive expansion across the state can be expected now that the holding company is established.[137]

On April 13, 1972, Union Planters reported that its first quarter operating earnings were $1.14 per share, down from $1.26 per share earned in 1971. Harrison "attributed the lower per-share figures to a decline in bond trading profits and the presence last year of a more favorable 'spread'—the difference between the bank's cost of money and rates at which it lends it out."[138]

On May 2, 1972, *The Commercial Appeal* reported that Harrison and Merkle would seek approval at the next board meeting of a new plan of organization that realigned senior bank officers:

> Basic to the new plan of organization is the creation of two new primary organizational units, the "banking group" (headed by T. A. Garrison) and the "support group" (headed by William B. Rudner). Each will report to the bank's president, James C. Merkle.
>
> The new banking group will oversee the corporate, retail banking and commercial loan divisions, as well as international accounts. The investment, operations, automation and planning divisions will report to the new support group.

Also reporting to the president under the plan is the new administrative division, which brings together the personnel, marketing and public relations functions of the bank, with L.A. Taylor, Jr. as division manager; and the trust division, headed by James F. Springfield.

Mr. Merkle said the "organization structure was realigned in a way that will significantly strengthen management efficiency and enhance the bank's long-term planning capabilities." Under the proposed plan, four group executives will report to the president, instead of nine.[139]

Also in May, Union Planters announced the opening of a new branch to be located in the Clark Tower. On July 1, 1972, the changeover to a one-bank holding company became effective. In the fall, management announced that it planned to acquire Percy Galbreath & Son, Inc., a mortgage banking firm which serviced approximately $180,000,000 in mortgages for 30 institutional investors. Under the plan, Union Planters National Bank would operate the mortgage banking firm as a subsidiary, and certain of the firm's operations, in which national banks were not permitted to operate, would be spun off and operated independently as The Galbreath Company.

In October of 1972, Union Planters opened the new Clark Tower branch. In November, Merkle (as incoming president of the Chamber of Commerce) launched the Chamber's "Believe in Memphis" program, stating, "Most Memphians are sold on their community and believe in it in varying degrees. But those who are timid about proclaiming its virtues are too often drowned out by others who are 'down on the town' or negative for one reason or another."[140] The Chamber of Commerce was trying diligently to solve the racial and economic problems that were surfacing in the city. Wallace Johnson, head of the "Believe in Memphis" campaign, stated:

This campaign will provide a podium from which we hope to erase the negativism that retards Memphis in many ways . . . .

We are not asking people to put on blinders concerning the problems we have as a community. What we are asking is that we think of these problems as the opportunities they really are for building an even finer city, for improving the quality of life of all citizens, and for helping Memphis attain new stature as a national and even as an international city.[141]

On November 26, 1972, Union Planters announced a new expansion strategy by offering trust services to the affluent suburbs at its White Station Tower Branch. Union Planters also continued its branch expansion strategy by announcing plans in December to open a new branch in the Germantown Mall. The bank also planned to continue its branch remodeling program. In an article published in the *Mid-Continent Banker*; Executive Vice President Garrison of Union Planters, stated:

If you want to keep a certain image in the community, you have to keep your place of business modern looking and fresh. . . . Extensive remodeling has given a face-lift to eight of Union Planters' 33 branches in the last year, and plans are underway for remodeling 10 more in 1973.[142]

Expansion through merger, using the newly created bank holding company, also became part of management's strategy:

Negotiations began late in the year with Tennessee National Bancshares, Inc., a registered bank holding company in Maryville, Tennessee [350 miles east of Memphis, near Knoxville], which, if consummated, would merge that company into Union Planters Corporation.

Tennessee National Bancshares became operative in September, 1971. Its two affiliates are the Blount National Bank in Maryville and the Merchants and Farmers Bank in Greenback, Tennessee. The two banks serve Loudon, Blount, and Monroe counties in East Tennessee.

Tennessee National Bancshares reported deposits of $56 million at the end of 1972 [5½% of Union Planters' total]. The proposed merger of the East Tennessee holding company into Union Planters Corporation is subject to the approval of certain regulatory authorities and shareholders of Tennessee National Bancshares, and other conditions.[143]

The financial statement of Union Planters Corporation for 1972 showed that earnings before net securities gains fell 10.3% from the prior year ($2.07 per share, versus $2.31 per share in 1971). Harrison and Merkle explained to shareholders, "The major cause for lower earnings in 1972 was an exceptionally large increase in the provision for loan losses which management considered necessary to maintain the valuation portion of the reserve for loan losses at an adequate level."[144] In prior years the loan loss reserve was provided, in effect, by a transfer from the bank's capital accounts; thus changes in the reserve had no effect on operating earnings. However, under Generally Accepted Accounting Principles, which the holding company was required to use in its financial reports, the provision for loan losses was charged to income and transferred to the loan loss reserve. In 1972, the provision of $4,206,815, up from $2,394,200 in 1971.[145]

However, earnings before securities gains in 1972 were $2.30 per share, compared with $2.36 per share in 1971, a decline of only 2.5%. Shareholders' equity increased by more than $4,000,000 to $77,225,599.[146] Operating income for 1972 increased by almost $7,400,000 to $58,785,032, but operating expenses increased by slightly more than $8,900,000 to $53,081,954. Of the $8,900,000 increase, $4,200,000 was required by the Loan Loss Reserve to reflect actual losses of approximately $4,400,000, up from $2,600,000 lost in the preceeding year.[147] Interest and dividends on investment securities continued to account for an increasing share of operating earnings. In 1971 income from investment securities provided 20.6% of total operating earnings. In 1972 the proportion rose to 23.7%. Interest and fees on loans were the source of 63.5% of 1972 operating earnings, approximately the same as in 1971 (63.4%); but service charges, trust fees, and all other income declined to 12.8% of total operating income in 1972, compared with 16.1% in 1971.[148]

Although the increased provision for loan losses produced a slight decline in earnings in 1972, as compared with 1971, Union Planters' management had reason for comfort. Peat, Marwick, Mitchell & Co. had been assisting management for more than a year, had examined operations over a two-year period, and was satisfied with the soundness of the results:

> Our examination was made in accordance with generally accepted auditing standards, and accordingly included such tests of the accounting records and such other auditing procedures as we considered necessary in the circumstances.
>
> In our opinion, such financial statements present fairly the financial position of Union Planters Corporation and subsidiaries at December 31, 1972 and 1971, the results of their operations, the changes in stockholder's equity, and the changes in financial position for the respective years then ended, in conformity with generally accepted accounting principles applied on a consistent basis.
>
> /s/ Peat, Marwick, Mitchell & Co.
>
> Memphis, Tennessee
> January 23, 1973[149]

6
CRISIS

As 1973 began, Memphis bankers were aware of the racial and economic problems faced by their region, but generally they remained optimistic. Union Planters continued to implement both its branch expansion strategy and its use of the newly formed holding company. During 1973 the bank opened one branch in Parkway Village and another in Raleigh Springs Mall, and it established a real estate loan operation at White Station Tower Branch, in addition to the Trust Department services added there earlier.[150] Union Planters also completed acquisition of the Galbreath mortgage banking firm on June 30, 1973, and reached agreement in May with Tennessee National Bankshares, Inc. (a small east Tennessee bank holding company) to merge that firm into Union Planters Corporation.[151]

Nevertheless, 1973 gradually turned into a nightmare for Union Planters. General economic conditions were not favorable, for interest rates climbed and money supplies tightened. However, independent of the economy, Union Planters suffered "a series of setbacks [in 1973], including a million dollar loss in its bond trading account, a $571,000 loss during the third quarter, unusually high losses in the installment credit department, a pending investigation of its investment division by the Securities and Exchange Commission, poor earnings prospects for the future, and personnel problems."[152] By November these "setbacks" were recognized as a major crisis. The agreement to merge with Tennessee National

Bankshares, Inc., "was terminated on November 15, 1973, because of adverse developments in the earnings of [Union Planters]" and on November 27, 1973, James C. Merkle, president of both the bank and the corporation, resigned.[153]

In announcing Merkle's resignation, Union Planters management issued only a four-paragraph statement devoid of details. Speculation existed that he might have been forced out because of the bank's poor operating performance and increasingly apparent problems. Although numerous articles about the resignation were published at the time, none cited a specific reason. A typical article noted that during Merkle's four years as president "the bank's total deposits have climbed from $638 million to more than $968.85 million, or more than 52%. And loans have soared from $377.5 million to $735.15 million."[154] But the article failed to note that the provision for loan losses had increased even faster than the loan portfolio during the same period.

Two months later, an article announcing Merkle's appointment as president and chief executive officer of the Bank of North Carolina and its parent company, Bankshares of North Carolina, stated: "He has told friends he left the Memphis bank because [he] was not allowed to make needed personnel and other changes."[155] Simultaneously, Union Planters formally announced the resignation to its stockholders "with regret," stating the "resignation was for personal reasons."[156] The day after Merkle's resignation, chairman of the board C. Bennett Harrison stated that the "house is in order . . . . We took all our lumps in the third quarter of this year. We now have our house in order, and the outlook is brighter."[157]

Merkle's resignation caused a reorganization of the bank's top management. Harrison temporarily assumed the duties of the president of the bank in addition to his duties as chairman of the board of both the bank and the holding company. William D. Galbreath, chairman of the board of Percy Galbreath & Sons, Inc. (a Union Planters subsidiary), became president of the holding company. On January 10, 1974, George C. Webb, vice chairman of the bank, also became its president.[158] In December, Garrison, the bank's executive vice president, resigned to accept a position as president of the First Marine Bank and Trust Company in Riviera Beach, Florida.[159] In the annual letter to the shareholders, Harrison and Galbreath stated:

> During 1973, the Commercial Loan Division of Union Planters National Bank of Memphis experienced the heaviest loan demand in its history. Loans outstanding at year end were $744,463,781 and averaged approximately $713 million for the year, an increase of 38% from the 1972 average balances. To finance this heavy loan demand for 1973 which lasted much longer than anticipated, it was necessary for the Bank to issue high interest-bearing certificates of deposit and to obtain funds from other banks at correspondingly high interest rates.
>
> Unfortunately, the high cost of funds in 1973 could not always be offset by increased interest charges on loans made by the Bank to its customers, since Tennessee law limits the maximum interest rates which may be charged . . . .
>
> Extraordinarily large unanticipated increases in the Bank's provision for loan losses during 1973 also had a substantial adverse impact on earnings. The provision for loan losses for 1973 was $7,045,358, which exceeded the 1972 provision by $2,827,318. Substantially all of this significant increase was deemed necessary as a result of unusually high recognized losses and anticipated losses in the Installment Credit Division of the Bank, principally attributable to automobile loans . . . . In general, the losses resulted from deficiencies in

the credit and collection functions of the Installment Credit Division . . . .

The [Bond Investment] Division's Trading Account sustained a loss of $305,529 in 1973, while Trading Account income for 1972 was $1,562,120. Substantially all of the Trading Account losses were incurred in the third quarter of 1973 when violations of a number of Bank policies were discovered by the Bank's internal auditors. During the fourth quarter of 1973, Trading Account operating income totaled $243,011.

Simultaneously with the discovery of the aforementioned losses, it was also learned that certain transactions involving the Trading Account had been improperly recorded for accounting purposes. As you are aware, two officers of the Bond Investment Division resigned and Bank personnel, assisted by its outside auditors, immediately commenced an intensive examination of Trading Account transactions. This examination disclosed that unreported net losses attributable to certain improperly recorded Trading Account transactions amounted to $93,800 for 1972 and $171,400 for 1971, which amounts are 1.3% and 2.4% respectively of the Corporation's reported net earnings for those years. It was also determined from this examination that certain securities classified as Trading Account securities in financial statements issued by the Bank for years prior to 1971 should have been classified as investment portfolio securities. In these financial statements, the Trading Account securities had been stated at cost in accordance with the Bank's accounting policy for the Trading Account at that time, and were not retroactively adjusted to the lower of cost or market which is the policy adopted in 1971 for that and subsequent years . . . .

Your officers and Directors are very much aware that 1973 was a disappointing year for both Management and shareholders. We assure you that significant improvements in controls and operating policies and practices were being implemented well before year-end. We continue to appreciate your support and encouragement and pledge to you that every effort will be made to prevent recurrence of problems and to strengthen the organization throughout.[160]

Union Planters charged off loans totaling approximately $6,500,000 in 1973,[161] an increase of nearly 50% over the almost $4,400,000 charged off in 1972. Because the dividend policy was not adjusted to reflect 1973 results, shareholder's equity fell to $78,524,703 by year end, a decrease of $97,134 during the year.[162] 1973 operating earnings (before net securities gains) fell to $0.89 per share, compared with $2.07 per share earned in 1972 (a decline of $1.18 per share, or 57%). However, of the $2,745,115 earned (before net securities gains) in 1973, all but $120,771 derived from income tax credits. Interest expense almost doubled over 1972 (to $51,401,756), and salaries increased by 20%. Although operating income increased by almost $27,000,000 during 1973, operating expenses increased by almost $33,000,000. Earnings before income taxes and net securities gains fell from $6,117,952 in 1972 to $120,771 in 1973, a decrease of 98%.[163]

Despite the crisis depicted in these financial reports and the major reversals in expected results for 1973, Union Planters had reason to expect that the crisis had passed. Peat, Marwick, Mitchell & Co. had worked another full year to assist the bank in overcoming internal control deficiencies. Although the problems in the bank's Installment Credit and Bond Investment Divisions had been uncovered by the bank's own people, Peat, Marwick, Mitchell & Co. had assisted in the resulting investigation. Management was able to assure shareholders "that significant improvements in controls and operating policies and practices were being implemented well before year-end."[164] Peat, Marwick once again had certified that it had conducted the tests and procedures it felt necessary to ensure itself that the 1973 "financial statements present fairly the financial position of Union Planters Corporation and subsidiaries . . . and the results of their operations and changes in their financial position . . . ."[165] Yet the crisis at Union Planters was far from over. In fact, the full extent of the difficulties were only beginning to unfold.

7
THE "INSIDE" STORY

To this point, the history of the rise and the beginning of the difficulties at the billion-dollar Union Planters National Bank have been developed through analysis of periodicals, books, newspaper articles, annual reports, and the records of the bank. The strategies of bank management, either stated or implicit in their actions, have been pieced together from statements in numerous publications and by observing the statistical history of the development of the institution. The economic, social, political, technological, and competitive factors which shaped management's decisions and strategies were synthesized from then-current literature. The results of management's various strategies became apparent through examination of the bank's financial statements and reports. But every organization has an inside story! What were the thoughts of personnel as the bank plunged into perilous times, and what were their views as to the reasons? One officer was particularly well-suited to provide the inside story. He is highly regarded by fellow employees, both old and new, for his analytical ability and his frankness, and he occupied strategic positions from which to observe the decline and the comeback of the bank. His name is James A. Gurley.

Gurley was first employed at Union Planters as a securities collection clerk in 1958, at age 25. In 1963 he was transferred to the General Books Department, where he maintained the general ledger for four years. In 1967 he left Union Planters to become the office manager and accountant for Royal Crown Cola Bottling Company's plants in Memphis and Mobile. In 1968, Union Planters asked Gurley to return to supervise its General Books Department and to implement a responsibility accounting system for the Bank. Gurley accepted and, in 1969, became a member of a special task force charged with designing and implementing a special accounting system for the Bank. He became head of the Bank's Accounting Department in 1970 and was promoted to accounting officer in 1971. The next year he was promoted to Assistant Controller, and later to Acting Controller. In the latter position he was responsible for some of the internal, external, and regulatory reporting of the bank, and he participated in evaluating loans to determine the adequacy of the bank's Loan Loss Reserve.

In 1974, Gurley assumed the duties of Cashier in addition to his responsibilities as Controller, and he was elevated to vice president of Loan Review and spent 12 months developing a practical system for reviewing loans. In 1975 he was placed in charge of the Special Loans Department, in addition to Loan Review. When the number of the bank's Special Loans (problem loans) increased dramatically, he was freed from his Loan Review responsibilities in order to focus his efforts on solving difficulties with problem loans. In 1977, the Real Estate Department and the Special Loans Department were merged into the Real Estate and Mortgage Loans Department. Gurley was named to head the new department.

Thus, Gurley served in several key positions which enabled him to appreciate not only the combination of factors which led to the bank's crisis, but also the various efforts which produced the miraculous turn-around. The remainder of this chapter summarizes the inside story for the period 1958 through 1973, as perceived by Gurley.[166]

During the late 1950s and early 1960s, Union Planters was considered "*The* Bank in the Mid-South." It achieved that status under Alexander, who built a bank much larger than any of its Memphis rivals. At that time, Union Planters viewed its only competition to be large banks located in Atlanta, Dallas, and St. Louis. John Brown, a country banker who became head of the largest bank in the Mid-South, continued the marketing strategy of his predecessor, Alexander, but he also implemented an authoritarian management style:

> Mr. Brown's management style was similar to that of a dictator, as compared to modern management styles. He made almost all of the important decisions in the bank and relinquished very little authority to other employees inside the bank. As a result, employee morale became low and the bank lost some personnel. These persons were replaced, at times, by persons who barely met the qualifications to perform the necessary functions, but who would do so at low salaries. As Mr. Brown was not management training program-oriented, no real attempt at developing a modern management training program was made.
>
> In managing the bank, Mr. Brown was very liquidity conscious and did not believe in high leverage investments for banking concerns.
>
> His marketing philosophy can be summarized by 'bigness will take care of us. We are the biggest bank in town with the largest branch system.' He obtained funds for the bank through correspondent banks, the large branch banking system and a few national accounts.
>
> In his lending practices, he was heavily dependent on the cotton business, security dealers business and the real estate business. He encouraged installment lending, but the emphasis was on obtaining the loans of Memphians who had a large net worth.
>
> Since Mr. Brown did not have a high regard for

management reporting systems, there were no checks and balances for loans such as a loan review committee. The loan committee could assist in controlling qualities of credit, but was not able to tell the quality of the loan officer to determine whether he had made the proper analysis of an adverse trend.[167]

Following Alexander's retirement in 1963, several economic, competitive, social, and political developments had a tremendous impact on the internal operations of the bank. Especially significant was the "overheated" economy of the loans, which produced a feeling within the business community that sustained rapid growth was both necessary and inevitable. Even executives of poorly managed businesses were able to benefit from the belief by most bankers, including Union Planters management, that "you couldn't make a bad loan." At Union Planters, unsound credit decisions and loose controls resulted from the frenetic effort to keep ahead of other banks—and numerous problem loans resulted. However, these problem loans were not recognized as such nor were they placed on a sound basis. They remained uncovered and were simply rolled over on the premise that "inflation will bail us out."

During the early 1960s, Union Planters' strongest, largest local competitor, the First National Bank of Memphis, shifted strategy and began to pursue a larger consumer base. As part of this effort, First National established a modern training program and built a young, aggressive management team. It also tried to project a corporate image as the "modern bank" in Memphis by completing a new, impressively modern, headquarters building which, kept blazing with lights at night, became a landmark on the downtown Memphis skyline. This gave First National even more visibility in the community. Additional competition for Union Planters occurred after Congress amended the Bank Holding Company Act in 1970. Nashville banks promptly reorganized within the framework of the Act and began to enter the Memphis market. First National also established a holding company and used it effectively. Union Planters delayed formation of a holding company until mid-1972, and became less able to compete on equal terms even in Memphis.

Legal restrictions also played an important role in the internal operation of the bank. For example, with passage of the Consumer Disclosure Act and the Consumer Protection Act, a huge amount of additional paperwork was created for banks. Although these acts increased the cost of credit to the consumer, many consumers paid little attention to the required disclosures and protections. Nevertheless, compliance was mandatory, and Union Planters was slow in implementing systems which could deal effectively with the increased paperwork. In addition, Tennessee's usury laws curtailed the earning power of Tennessee banks by preventing them from competing with financial institutions located in other states; out-of-state lenders were generally not restricted by Tennessee's interest ceiling, but Tennessee lenders were.

Another important factor affecting the operations of the bank grew out of society's increasing emphasis on youth. It became fashionable for top management to recruit, hire, and depend on "young turks"—new university graduates drenched in modern theories of business but with little banking experience, who preached that leverage was the answer to greater profits, that inflation would bail management out of any problems, and that "if the REITs (Real Estate Investment Trusts) can do it, why can't we." Union Planters' top management ultimately adopted the theory that "if one young turk knows modern ways of doing business and increasing profits, let's capitalize by hiring more of them." At Union Planters, the young turks were great planners. Their plans, however, often were implemented by clerks who understood neither the purpose of the plans nor how to coordinate their elements; and, most important, they did not know how to implement their plans successfully. Ultimately, competition built among the young turks to conceive and develop new plans in order to progress within the organization. Because the various plans competed against rather than complemented each other, the result was chaos.

Upon succeeding to the leadership of the bank, Harrison utilized a different management style:

> Mr. Harrison attempted to build an organizational structure with management depth, but the situation was out of control due to people in various managerial positions and the lack of proper controls. Unlike Mr. Brown, Mr. Harrison believed in delegating authority. But he delegated too much authority and positions within the bank were heavily influenced by internal politics rather than job qualifications.
>
> Mr. Harrison employed Mr. Merkle whose job was to organize the bank. Both Mr. Harrison and Mr. Merkle wanted to be the head of a bank that is nationally known. Consequently, they focused on growth. Their marketing philosophy could be summarized as leverage to the hilt: 'If you get the growth, the profits will come.'
>
> Unfortunately, the operating system was inadequate for implementation of such a philosophy, and the accounting system provided very little information for managerial decision-making. We developed a "responsibility accounting system" and "Jerry-rigged" other systems to feed it. Even with the 'jerry-rigging,' the system would have worked except for one important factor: The managers had educated the employees below them to be mechanical rather than innovative. The new system was not well understood by the employees, and ultimately led to a breakdown as

well as lack of confidence in the bank's financial control system.

During 1971, there was a reduction in the demand for funds and the bank emphasized real estate loans to obtain volume. Ultimately, this was disastrous due to inadequate analysis of projects by bankers who were not real estate experts; the use of the funds was not well documented in all cases; and the bank had very little control over construction draws.

Thus, the organization structure of the bank was not readily understood, and the bank's financial control system lacked employee confidence. Meanwhile, growth-oriented management continued to develop innovative marketing ideas.

The "Your Name Is Your Collateral" campaign is one of the most outstanding examples of a communications breakdown. Top management's idea was not total unsecured lending; rather, to let the public realize that Union Planters believed in the consumer, and that one's reputation and name were important. The communication of this approach was somehow misunderstood. The result of the communication breakdown was fiasco for the bank.[168]

The recession that occurred in the early 1970s eventually forced management to recognize what had happened. Union Planters was not alone, however, for the entire banking industry was confronted with severe problems. But those problems were compounded at Union Planters by severe internal problems: poor controls, a multitude of effects resulting from bad decision-making, excessive lending, lack of organization and supervision, and ineffective management generally. That combination of external and internal problems not only threatened the bank's existence, but also made successful solutions much more difficult to find and to implement:

In relating the various leadership styles, managerial philosophies and strategies of the presidents and chairmen of the board during this period, it must be stated that to the best of my knowledge each man was completely loyal and gave his best efforts in leading the bank within the set of conditions that he inherited as he assumed these positions. The combination of the individual leaders frame of reference, inability of an organization to respond as quickly as was sometimes needed, the legacy of directing the Mid-South's largest bank with the accompanying pressures to maintain that position and the prevailing conditions within our economy—all were important evolutionary ingredients whose combination led to the precipitation of crisis.[169]

Merkle's resignation during the crisis of 1973 required Union Planters' to search for unusually qualified New Leadership. Fortunately the bank found it.

8
NEW LEADERSHIP

Following Merkle's resignation, the top echelon at Union Planters continued to undergo reorganization. On January 10, 1974, the board of directors appointed George C. Webb president. Webb had been employed by the bank for 26 years and had served as vice chairman of the board since 1972. He was well acquainted both with the bank's internal operations and with the top men at Union Planters' correspondent banks. Harrison described the new president's duties in an interview at the time: "Webb will work closely with [me] in directing the day-to-day activities of the bank. He also will be active in the business and economic development areas, plus the trust division."[170] Webb's appointment was obviously only a stop-gap move by Union Planters' board, for Webb was 63 years of age, and the bank had a policy of mandatory retirement at age 65. Also, no one was appointed to replace Webb as vice chairman when he became the bank's 18th president.

On May 13, 1974, the board decided to bring an outsider into Union Planters' top echelon instead of promoting someone from within. William M. Matthews was named president of the Union Planters Corporation (the holding company parent of the bank), succeeding William D. Galbreath. A native of Decatur, Georgia, Matthews originally aspired to be a Wall Street investment banker. He entered commercial banking in 1956 on the advice of his uncle, who suggested he should first acquire that background. After a tour of active duty in

William M. Matthews, Jr., Chairman & Chief Executive Officer of Union Planters National Bank 1974—.

the army, Matthews applied for a job at two banks and was hired by First National of Atlanta. First of Atlanta was trying to recover from declining prestige, and had recently hired a new chairman who had implemented an administrative training program. Matthews entered the new program as an administrative trainee. Approximately three years later, he became an assistant cashier. On completing the training program, he requested a transfer to the bank's investment department where he became a security analyst. Three years after that, Matthews became a vice president and was portfolio manager for corporate and individual accounts. As part of these duties, he wrote a Report to the U.S. Steel Pension Fund. Although Matthews did not recognize it at the time, this report was the catalyst that accelerated his banking career.

The chairman of the First National Bank of Atlanta, James D. Robinson, read Matthews' report and was favorably impressed. In 1966, Robinson personally asked Matthews to help a management consulting firm prepare a written organizational and marketing manual for the bank. The ensuing study, which was undertaken to improve the bank's efficiency as well as to organize the firm so that it could readily adapt emerging technological advances, took one and one-half years to complete. In June of 1967, First of Atlanta began to implement the recommendations produced by the study. Robinson, the bank's chairman, died one month later. Although he did not live to see the study successfully implemented, Robinson had a considerable influence on Matthews' career by giving him corporate visibility. Robinson also provided the leadership style and example which has continued to influence Matthews throughout his banking career.

In 1967, Matthews was appointed head of the money management division of the bank. Two years later, he was elected a senior vice president and director of the bank's portfolio investments operation and investment services. In 1971, he was elected executive vice president of the bank's holding company, First National Holding Corporation. Matthews became president of the holding company in 1972, and remained in that position until 1974 when he moved to Memphis as president of the Union Planters Corporation.

> In the spring of 1974 he [Matthews] became disenchanted and made up his mind to leave his job. So, when directors and influential Union Planters stockholders approached him about the presidency there, he was receptive. However, it was a trip to Paris that same spring that convinced him to take the Memphis job.
> He spent a week in the French capital at a Young Presidents Organization world outlook conference. The principal long-range problem identified by the conference was world food production. "There is no better [agricultural] area in the country than the area surrounding Union Planters," Mr. Matthews said. "I thought I would be able to contribute more, to accomplish more here than any place in the country. That is what made up my mind."[171]

Upon joining Union Planters, Matthews quickly concluded that he would not be able to devote his total efforts to the holding company. The problems of the subsidiary, Union Planters National Bank, were substantially greater than he had anticipated, and these could not be solved simply by installing management controls.

The biggest immediate problem confronting the president of the holding company was to get the bank's balance sheet "under control." Matthews analyzed the bank's loan control system and recognized that it was not adequate. For example, Union Planters was losing too much money through customer's overdrafts. Part of the continuing loan problem stemmed from the bank's unstated policy that "any loan officer could commit the bank's legal limit." Further, because of prevailing interest rates and Tennessee's 10% usury ceiling, bank personnel were making "prime rate" loans to numerous businesses and individuals who did not have the credit standing to qualify for such treatment. The ultimate result of these policies was that "Union Planters was taking the risk instead of the borrowers to whom management loaned money."[172]

In an effort to learn more about the organization of the bank and to familiarize top management with his philosophies, Matthews formed the "UP Team." This team, which consisted of the top two levels of management in the bank, met in the evenings in an informal atmosphere to discuss the bank's existing organization and operating procedures. These meetings enabled Matthews to glean the employees' impressions of the bank and of the problems which existed both within and between the various departments. After several UP Team meetings and additional conversations with the bank's branch managers and other employees, Matthews concluded that the internal problems of Union Planters were: (1) In general, Union Planters' employees did not understand the operations of the bank, and would not recommend it to new customers. (2) Union Planters' tellers were performing bookkeeping functions which slowed their performance and cost the bank money. Furthermore, although the bank had recently purchased two IBM 370s, it did not have proper computer audit controls. (3) Branch managers were not business-oriented and did not understand their responsibilities. Four layers of management existed between the branch managers and the top administrative decision-makers, and communications and morale problems prevailed. (4) None of the branch managers assumed the responsibility for making any of the "Your Signature is Your Collateral" loans. Branch managers were caught up in administrative paperwork and did not understand the proper method of making loans. And (5), the UP Team discussions confirmed that Union Planters did not have the necessary control systems for existing loan volume. The liability ledger of the bank was organized in such a manner that it was impossible to determine whether one loan was related to another. Management had a list of loans, but could not identify concentrations of credit, account profitability, or whether loans were duplicative or at cross-purposes. Consequently, no employee of Union Planters knew what the bank's total exposure was.[173]

Thus Matthews had left a comfortable position at one of Atlanta's finest banks to take over the reins of a billion dollar banking institution, but one which was unorganized and riddled with problems that might well prove to be fatal. When he came, Matthews had promised the board of directors that he would keep as many existing employees as possible when reorganizing the bank. Later he said, "If I had known what I was getting into, I never would have come. But I was here. Because of my family and my ego, I would have to make the best of the situation."[174] And the situation was shockingly critical.

In addition to the grave internal problems (which were not publicly known), Union Planters had gotten involved in a publicized lawsuit stemming from the sale of the 100 North Main Building. Union Planters had financed construction of the building and ended up owning it after the project ran into problems involving cost overruns and withdrawal of permanent mortgage commitments. Union Planters finally sold the building to Massachusetts Mutual Life Insurance Company on terms which permitted the bank to retain its branch operation on the first floor of the building and to continue to have its landmark sign atop the structure. In announcing the sale of the building on July 10, 1974,

Harrison stated, "The sale substantially reduces the bank's investment in real estate and provides capital for other investment activities, plus greater flexibility for future planning. Some of the money will be used to meet continuing high loan demand."[175] Approximately one month later, the original developer of the building (BBI, Inc.) filed a $30,000,000 damage suit in Chancery Court charging that Union Planters, the Galbreath Company, and others had conspired to defraud BBI and its stockholders by "using interlocking directorships." Although the size of the lawsuit caused unwarranted and unwanted publicity, Union Planters was not overly concerned. Management felt the lawsuit would be dismissed at an early stage once the facts were developed.

Despite this lawsuit, Union Planters' top management recognized it needed to devote the overwhelming majority of its time to solving its internal problems. It was imperative to determine the total exposure of the bank and to develop a sound loan control system. Only then could the bank focus on profits. Matthews had installed an Account Profitability Analysis system at the First National Bank of Atlanta, but he was uncertain whether existing Union Planters personnel were capable of handling such a system. This system, which ultimately would prove extremely important to the bank, produces an analysis of the actual profit contribution of a particular customer (all income derived from the customer minus all expenses incurred for the customer) which then can be compared with account profitability forecasts and goals set by management. Such a system would permit Union Planters to: (1) improve the profitability of individual customers and (ultimately) the bank as a whole; (2) modify the bank's loan portfolio to emphasize more profitable loans; (3) enhance management's ability to meet competition; (4) furnish quantitative guidelines to describe, implement, and evaluate policy; (5) evaluate loan officer performance; and (6) permit the bank to move in the direction of profit-oriented marketing efforts.

Confronted with "surprises" almost daily during his first two and one-half months, Matthews sought to create a "no surprise" environment at Union Planters. In August of 1974 he established a Special Loans Department, to be staffed by people with sufficient expertise to solve problem loans of any size and dimension. The department was to be organized so that its personnel could look at problems and make decisions objectively, for they were not the loan officers who had made the loans originally. The department's existence also made borrowers realize that Union Planters not only was serious about solving its problem loans, but also capable of doing it. The initial task for Special Loans was to go through every problem loan in the bank; that is, any loan which had been criticized by the federal bank examiners, any loan which had shown a large loss recently, and any loan which was past due. Each problem loan was analyzed by inspecting the original documents. If necessary, legal counsel was employed to determine the bank's security position. Then a meeting was held with the problem loan customer to determine if the customer had sufficient financial resources to eliminate the loan from the problem category. Special Loans officers also considered the borrower's interest in solving the problem, his integrity, his spirit of cooperation, and his expertise in performing the function for which the loan was made. Based on an analysis of these factors, Special Loans decided either to develop a workout plan with the borrower or else to initiate legal proceedings to liquidate collateral and collect any deficiency from those liable to repay the loan.

Although the logic employed in developing the Special Loan concept approach and operating procedures appeared simple, management had difficulty im-

plementing it. The first difficulty incurred was to identify people in the bank who were suited for a position in
this department: people who could monitor several loans
in different industries, who could function well in crisis
situations, who could operate in a discouraging environment, and who were capable of making sound judgments
both on complicated legal issues and on serious business
problems. Another difficulty encountered was deter-
mining when (and how much) expensive legal assistance
should be hired to help the bank reach an accurate decision in each case. The most difficult problem encountered, however, was in developing sufficient controls
over the myriad responsibilities which Special Loans had
to undertake. For example, if Union Planters had to take
over real estate projects which were between 10 and 90
percent complete, how could it fund and hire the necessary consultants and contractors to complete and market
the projects; and how could their activities be effectively
utilized, monitored, and controlled? The responsibilities
of Special Loans personnel ranged from banker to manager of several different kinds of development projects
and businesses. Rudolph Holmes, recognized by management for his outstanding efforts in attempting to
solve the bank's installment loan problem, was chosen to
organize and manage a new Loan Administration Division, which later included the Special Loans department.

While management was quietly reorganizing the
bank, the public, and members of the banking industry
and financial community in particular, were becoming
increasingly aware of the bank's problems by analyzing
the published quarterly financial statements. On August
12, 1974, the *American Banker* reported:

> Union Planters Corp., severely plagued last year by
> installment loan problems in its anchor bank, Union
> Planters National Bank, has been hit with heavy real
> estate loan problems in the most recent quarter.
> The latest loan problems of the $1.25 billion asset

holding company sent it deep into red ink for the second quarter. It reported a net loss, after modest securities transaction gains, of $9,798,065—the equivalent of $3.19 per share. A year earlier, it had a second quarter net profit, also after modest securities gains, of $1,500,999 or $.49 a share.

At June 30, the bank stopped accruing interest on $25 million in real estate related loans, and said last week that there is a high probability that it will foreclose on some in the near future.

It wrote off $4 million in loans—largely real estate related—at the end of the second quarter and added $10 million to its provisions for loan losses during that quarter.

The second quarter loss stemmed principally from the increase in the provision for loan losses in order to maintain the reserve for loan losses at an adequate level, Union Planters said.

William M. Matthews, Jr., who assumed the post of president and chief executive officer of the holding company last June, said that the loans written off in the second quarter were largely real estate loans to concerns whose financial conditions deteriorated sharply during the quarter.

The $894.9 million-deposit bank anticipated that the increase in the reserve for loan losses will cover losses which may be incurred in connection with the loans on which it stopped accruing interest. Foreclosures would not increase the losses for which provision has been made, it said.

Tennessee's 10% usury ceiling, too, adversely affected the holding company. The bank estimated that its revenues for the six months ended June 30, would have been increased by some $7 million to $10 million if it had been legally permitted to charge prevailing national interest rates on its loan portfolio.[176]

During this period of constant adverse publicity for Union Planters, the new leader of the problem-plagued banking institution made two decisions which turned the bank's notoriety to its advantage. Matthews piqued interest locally by purchasing a 9000-square-foot landmark home with a ballroom, billiard room, sauna, swimming pool, and other accessories. Needless to say, that investment by the chief executive of a banking institution labeled as having "grave problems" started tongues wagging in the community, but it also suggested that Matthews—and, by inference, Union Planters—were there to stay. Matthews' second action brought him national recognition in the banking industry. Searching for ways to obtain a higher return on loans despite Tennessee's 10% usury limit, Matthews conceived the idea of tying the principal of a loan to the consumer price index in order to eliminate the effect of changing price levels (inflation or deflation) on both borrower and lender. Thus the bank would get back principal of equal purchasing power to that which it loaned, and inflation, by cheapening money, would neither produce a windfall for the borrower nor erode the loan's asset value to the bank. The bank made such an indexed loan to Aztec Properties, Inc. Aztec repaid the principal and 10% interest, but refused to pay the additional principal called for by the index clause. Union Planters sued. The concept and the lawsuit received national recognition in *The Wall Street Journal, Business Week,* and *American Banker.*

Acting conservatively, Union Planters sought to obtain a favorable ruling from the Tennessee Supreme Court before making indexed loans a common practice. (The Tennessee Supreme Court ultimately ruled against Union Planters.) Meanwhile, bank management worked with other Tennessee bankers to obtain Congressional passage of the Brock Bill, an amendment to the federal banking laws which would provide temporary relief from Tennessee's usury laws.

On October 17, 1974, C. Bennett Harrison resigned, whereupon Union Planters' board of directors selected

Matthews chairman and chief executive officer of both the bank and the holding company. Richard Trippeer, an active young board member, was selected president of the bank, replacing George Webb (scheduled for retirement in 13 months at age 65), who was elevated to vice chairman of the bank. Commenting on his retirement, Harrison stated, "Due to the vast changes the banking industry is undergoing, I considered it important that Union Planters have a completely new and younger executive leadership. I think the holding company and bank are in excellent hands under Mr. Matthews and Mr. Trippeer."[177]

Union Planters Corporation simultaneously announced a loss for the third quarter of $2,796,561, or $.91 per share, although operating earnings were positive. For the first nine months in 1974 the holding company reported a net loss of $11,871,787, or $3.87 per share, compared with net income of $.84 per share during the first ninth months in 1973.[178] A local newspaper reported comments by Trippeer, the new president, on the bank's financial situation and on Matthews' leadership:

> Our operating earnings are now positive, and we think passage of the Brock Bill will further enhance our profitability . . . .
> No further shakeup in management personnel will be forthcoming. I am the last member of the team to be assembled by Mr. Matthews . . . .
> Steps have already been taken to improve that profit picture, although the bank still needs to run leaner, harder and faster.
> The economy has worsened. That, plus the tight money situation and the large portfolio of real estate that we had, meant the bank just had to get hurt.
> He stressed that he was not "throwing stones" at any previous management, but he added that since Matth-

ews took the helm in June, the company has already taken significant steps to reduce the impact of lowered interest margins, the difference between the bank's high cost of money, and the interest it was able to charge customers.

Some of these steps include a reduction of loan levels from $737.3 million to $723 million and a further reduction as of last Tuesday to $686.6 million. Investment securities were reduced from $260.9 million to $221.1 million and an office building was sold for $10.5 million. Negotiable certificates of deposits were reduced by $79.1 million.

These actions resulted in an improvement in operating results by some $400,000.[179]

Thus, Union Planters' top management consisted of an experienced banker who had been with the firm for only five months and an active young board member with no other banking experience. It would be the responsibility of these two people to keep Union Planters' billion dollar doors open despite its overwhelming problems.

KEEPING THE DOORS OPEN

At the time he assumed the leadership of Union Planters, Matthews' immediate objective was to secure adequate control over the balance sheet. Obtaining the desired control proved unexpectedly difficult. This chapter discusses the numerous interrelated surprises, complex problems, and events that confronted the new chief executive officer in his first seven and one-half months at Union Planters, and it describes the various actions taken to negotiate the maze of hazards which arose.

Matthews focused immediately on the bank's operational and organizational deficiencies and on restructuring the bank's loan portfolio to reduce the profit-sapping impact of prevailing money market conditions. Matthews' biggest surprise—and the bank's primary problem—surfaced somewhat later. The major cause of the bank's losses and the most serious threat to its continued existence turned out to be employee infidelity. It was only after suspicions of dishonesty arose in late summer of 1974 that Matthews' attention was diverted to that problem.

On May 13, 1974, Matthews' first day at Union Planters, he was informed that the Securities and Exchange Commission (SEC) was threatening to sue Union Planters National Bank for alleged material omissions from required financial reports, and that the proposed complaint might name at least two former officers. The settlement which Matthews ultimately negotiated with the

SEC became both an important precedent and a lesson in internal operations and procedures for the banking industry. The novelty and potential significance of the settlement was discussed in an important *Law Review* article:

A slightly different but nonetheless novel approach was incorporated in the consent decree in *SEC v. Union Planters Corp.*. In this case, a bank holding company, its principal bank, a broker-dealer, and various individuals allegedly engaged in a fraudulent scheme in violation of §10(b) and Rule 10b-5 of the 1934 Act. The alleged scheme principally related to improper valuations and sales of securities in the bank's investment and trading accounts.

Specifically, the SEC's complaint charged that securities which had declined in value since their original purchase were transferred from the Bank's securities trading account to its securities investment account. Since the bank valued securities in the investment account at original cost, no downward valuation or write-down occurred. The SEC further alleged that the various defendants created an arrangement whereby the Bank from time to time would sell certain securities to the broker-dealer at prices in excess of the market value of the securities. Such transactions enabled the Bank either to conceal losses which otherwise would have occurred or to report inflated trading account profits. At the same time, the Bank entered into an arrangement with the broker-dealer to repurchase the securities at a later time and to guarantee the broker-dealer against any losses on the transactions.

To settle this case, the defendant consented to court-ordered undertakings in lieu of injunctions against future violations of the anti-fraud provisions of the 1934 Act. In addition, the bank holding company and the Bank undertook to establish certain procedures to prevent future violations, which were incorporated in the court order. The undertakings are lengthy, but deserve consideration in their entirety because of their novelty and potential significance. They include the following:

1. The preparation and circulation not less frequently than semi-annually to each officer, trader or salesman in the Investment Division of an extract of the applicable current Rules of Fair Practice of the NASD;

2. The review of the Investment Division, at least annually, under the direction and guidance of the chief administrative officer of the Company, with the advice and assistance of his chief financial officer and legal counsel, to insure that its policies and procedures with respect to both the Trading Account and Investment Account and the legal, accounting and record keeping requirements and procedures in the Division and its Operations Department are in compliance with applicable law;

3. The preparation of written guidelines to Trading Account and Investment Account policies including: types of securities, general mix of securities, maximum underwriting positions, reporting of losses, valuation procedures, reporting slow moving inventory, concessions on purchases and sales, forbidden transactions and approvals and review of transactions;

4. The written confirmation by the officers, traders and salesmen in the Investment Division of the trading and investment policies and guidelines;

5. The preparation and circulation to all appropriate personnel of a detailed statement of accounting policies and requirements for security transactions within the Investment Division, account, investment account, and special situations such as: short sales, arbitrage transactions, commercial paper and money market activity including federal funds, securities sold under agreements to repurchase, securities purchased under agreements to resell,

and certificates of deposits sold to New York banks;

6. The implementation of a continuing training program for the Investment Division's personnel, including a periodic review of previously established policies;

7. The continuous review by the Manager of the Investment Division, with the advice of counsel, of legal developments relating to applicable securities activities and the dissemination of legal advice defining illegal activities, including free riding to all personnel in the Investment Division and periodic confirmation of such personnel that any employee is subject to immediate dismissal who (1) engaged in any practice or activity which is either illegal or contrary to established bank policy or procedures or (2) invests personally, whether directly or indirectly, in any security other than with the limitations established by the Division without the specific approval of the Manager;

8. The monthly reporting by the Operations Department of the Investment Division, with responsibility for the orderly handling of paperwork, book entries and the implementation in that Division of the Bank's accounting policies and requirements, to both the Manager of the Bond Investment Division and the Bank's Financial Division;

9. The maintenance as soon as practicable hereafter of the books and records of the Investment Division relating to all securities transactions and positions in accordance with the applicable provisions of Regulation 240.17a-3 under Section 17 of the Exchange Act;

10. The establishment of a management committee to include at least three outside directors of the Bank to supervise specifically the Investment Division and transactions involving its Investment Account and Trading Account, which Committee shall meet at least monthly and shall submit to the Board of Directors regular reports on the status and operations of that Division.

This case has two noteworthy features. The first is the internal procedures and controls which the Bank agreed to adopt. The procedures are quite extensive and relate directly to the internal operations of a national bank which is subject to extensive regulation by federal banking authorities. From the standpoint of regulatory agency jurisdiction, one must wonder why these internal procedures and improvements were not mandated by banking authorities rather than in the context of settlement of an SEC enforcement case. Traditionally, banks have objected vociferously to any efforts by the SEC to exert jurisdiction over banking matters, even in such less controversial areas as bank stock transfer agent operations. The intrusion of the SEC into the internal operations and procedures of a bank in the context of a Rule 10b-5 proceeding potentially represents greater substantive SEC control over banks than many authorities have ever imagined.

The second significant factor of the *Union Planters* settlement is that no injunction was entered. In lieu of injunctions embodying the foregoing procedures as mandatory relief, the Bank agreed to court-ordered undertakings in lieu of injunctions which were made part of the court order. Since this case was settled by consent, the order contains no explanation of the rationale supporting the use of undertakings as opposed to injunctions. A between-the-lines analysis of the complaint and the final decree gives rise to one possibility. That possibility is that the alleged fraudulent scheme was essentially an individual frolic by some of its officers and employees, lacking the approval, condonation or even knowledge of the senior officers and directors of the Bank. If so, this may have been the bargaining tool which convinced the SEC to settle on the basis of undertakings, which seemingly constitute less of a stigma than injunctions.

It is interesting to note that no provision of the '33 or '34 Acts refers to undertakings or to any power of the SEC to seek compliance with undertakings by way of motions for contempt citations. However, it seems highly unlikely that the SEC would accede to such a settlement unless it were confident that it could compel compliance. This apparent power, coupled with the fact that the Bank continues to be subject to internal regulation by banking authorities, may well have been the controlling factors in dictating this unique settlement.[180]

On arriving at Union Planters, Matthews' immediate impression was that the bank had a number of organizational and operational problems, of which control was only one. His review of the bank's financial statements showed that the bank's loan portfolio was supported by a disproportionately high percentage of interest-sensitive funds. Union Planters was *paying* well over 10% for interest-sensitive funds but, because of Tennessee's usury laws, the bank could *receive* only 10% on the vast majority of the loans it was able to make. *THUS, AS UNION PLANTERS' INCREASED ITS LOAN PORTFOLIO, IT LOST INCREASING AMOUNTS OF MONEY.*

Matthews' first actions were directed toward the money-market. Because no one at Union Planters knew the total exposure of the bank or whether dangerous concentrations of credit existed, he quickly directed that no further overdrafts would be permitted. Although implementation of this order resulted in complaints from bank customers, it prevented further losses from carrying overdrafts with funds which cost the bank more than it was able to charge its customers for the overdraft privilege.

In order to obtain a better understanding (for both the bank and himself) of Union Planters' loan position, Matthews created a Loan Administration Division. The Division's first duties were to review all loans in the bank's portfolio to determine their quality and to establish controls to insure that all future loans would be of proper quality. Loan Review also developed a numerical risk-rating for all credits ("one" for lowest risk loans and "five" for most risky). Along with the risk-ranking system, the Division also implemented Matthews' Account Profitability Analysis program. All large (over $100,000) loan and deposit accounts were formally reviewed to see which were profitable to the bank. All loans (and all other allocated capital) were ranked, and the rankings were used to create a profitability index of the bank's customer base.

Using the Account Profitability Analysis system, Matthews was able to identify all unprofitable accounts. The system also disclosed that a disproportionately high concentration of funds had been loaned to a narrow group of bank customers. In June of 1974, approximately 15% of Union Planters' entire loan portfolio—almost $100,000,000—had been loaned to only eight borrowers and their related interests. It was later determined that three of those eight borrowers were involved in the infidelity of some of the bank's officers. Matthews also noted that a Union Planters account officer was responsible not only for selling the bank's services, including loans, but also was responsible for approving and reviewing the customer's credit. This meant, in effect, that account officers were the only persons who monitored their own activities. Although this method was an acceptable (indeed a common) banking practice, Matthews thought it necessary to separate the two functions; he wanted account officers neither to set prices nor to make financial decisions. The responsibilities of account officers soon were limited to calling on the bank's large deposit accounts, ascertaining credit needs, and relaying those needs to an appropriate loan officer. The loan officer then assumed responsibility for the quality of the credit—if the loan was made.

In order to communicate basic responsibilities to bank officers, management formalized an officers' code of ethics. Non-officer employees were encouraged to become familiar with the code and to abide by its principals and provisions, but the code was made binding only on bank officers. The code's focus on expected conduct was later refined into a contract system. Management level employees were required periodically to execute formal undertakings with the bank and to perform in acceptable ways and at acceptable levels. This approach was an innovation which proved of major importance in the survival of Union Planters.

Matthews learned that prior to his arrival the bank had experienced unusually large losses in consumer installment loans, had promptly notified regulatory authorities, and had launched a thorough investigation of the installment credit department. Matthews intensified this investigation in July of 1974. He asked that all installment credit personnel be polygraphed. As a result of these tests and others, he became convinced that crimes had been committed. The investigation revealed that certain employees had received payments from retailers and customers in return for approving credit applications. Management also found out that some loans on the books had been made to individuals who either did not exist or could not be located.

Dishonesty in the installment loan department of Union Planters cost the bank at least $5,400,000. This made it imperative to develop an installment loan system with safeguards to prevent tampering with the aging of receivables. Among other things, the system had to be complete and accurate, immediately pinpoint any loan that went without a payment for a specified period of time, and indicate the amount and date of the last payment made to the account. Further, a procedure for routinely screening approved credit applications to determine their quality and to keep track of Union Planters' market share of credit applications had to be developed.

Matthews proceeded to ensure that all of this was promptly implemented.

During the last week in August and the first week in September of 1974, federal bank examiners visited Union Planters. A senior loan officer asked Matthews not to show them the "white list" (a list of concentrations of credit and numerous problem loans which had been revealed by the Accounts Profitability system) or "they will close the bank."[181] Matthews ignored the request, and reviewed the white list with the federal bank examiners.

In September of 1974, the embezzlement of bank funds by a former branch manager was discovered through normal loan review procedures. The discovery led to another thorough investigation which revealed that the former officer had made loans to certain parties on whom no credit history (or any other information) could be found. When questioned, he was unable to provide management with any information that could be verified. Several weeks later he admitted that he had made a number of fictitious loans. The loss from these loans alone was in excess of $225,000.

In addition to the embezzlement, the investigation also revealed that this same individual was responsible for an enormous credit exceeding $10,000,000. Routine loan review procedures yielded no meaningful credit information on the company involved. Although the branch manager responsible for the loan had resigned from Union Planters prior to Matthews' arrival, management questioned him regarding the loan. The former manager refused information on the grounds that the company was under investigation by the Internal Revenue Service (IRS), and he could not release financial information until that investigation had been completed. As a result of this embezzlement and questions regarding the $10,500,000 loan, Union Planters' management began to strengthen certain controls to include the independent review and audit both of loan information and of any large amounts of cash leaving the bank.

In October of 1974, Matthews began to implement a *new* branch system. He had concluded that Union Planters (with 36 branch operations) was over-branched. From conversations with the bank's branch managers, Matthews also had concluded that they understood neither banking operations nor the duties and responsibilities of a branch manager. Matthews explained his philosophy to the branch managers:

> Although the normal retail customer represents ninety percent of the bank's accounts, this group is only responsible for ten to twenty percent of the bank's deposits. The larger accounts, approximately ten percent of the bank's total accounts, are responsible for eighty to ninety percent of total deposits. The purpose of advertising is to get people into the bank. It is the responsibility of the branch manager to know his retail customers and to assist them in their loan service requirements. The branch manager should be at his desk between 11:30 a.m. and 1:30 p.m., for that is the time when most customers come to see him. In addition to these duties, the branch manager is responsible for handling the personnel problems in his branch and its teller efficiency.[182]

Studying the efficiency of then-existing operating procedures, Matthews found that Union Planters' tellers were averaging only 150 transactions per day, but should be averaging 400. This difference in performance was due to an antiquated system which utilized duplicate deposit slips. Matthews also discovered that correspondent bank accounting was taking eight to nine hours per day under the existing system. A bank should complete its correspondent bank's accounting in six to seven hours.

Union Planters' 36 branches had been divided into quadrants with four regional managers reporting to Branch Administration. Matthews wanted to restructure the bank's branch operation, but came to the conclusion that only eight of the 36 branch managers would be able to operate under a new system. The branch operation concept envisioned by Matthews included only 24 branches: Eight "A" branches would make their own decisions, handle credits up to a million dollars, and be responsible for sub-branches; eight "B" branches would be "full service" branches; and eight "C" branches would only take loan applications and cash checks. The other existing branches were to be phased out as soon as possible. The first steps in implementing the program were made in 1974, but Matthews' restructuring was not completed until the middle of 1976.

After Harrison resigned in October of 1974, Matthews was named chairman of the board and chief executive officer both of the holding company and the bank; Richard Trippeer became president of the bank; Jessie Barr continued to head the Banking area; Rudolph Holmes administered Loan Administration, including Loan Review and Special Loans; Harry Maihafer was in charge of the Personnel Department; James A. Cook was the chief financial officer; and William B. Rudner was responsible for discussing the bank's financial condition with investment analysts and wealthy customers. Rudner also was responsible for civic affairs and public relations with the Memphis community. Benjamin Rawlins, a computer expert from Atlanta, became head of the Operations Division. Rawlins' chief responsibility was redesigning computer programs to enhance operating efficiency and to protect against theft by developing computer audit controls. The accounting firm of Price Waterhouse & Co. assisted Rawlins in a consulting capacity. A Georgia bank president, William Dick, was employed by Union

Richard A. Trippeer, Jr., President, Union Planters National Bank 1974—.

Planters to supervise one large problem with concentrated credits—loans to Stax Record Company and its related entities. These changes were effected before the public fireworks began.

On November 5, 1974, an article appeared in *The Commercial Appeal* entitled "Probe is Linked to Bank Losses." Although it was known that Union Planters had some problems, the general public now began to learn of their severity:

> The Federal Grand Jury yesterday began an investigation apparently related to substantial 1973 losses in the bond trading operations of Union Planters National Bank.
>
> The nature of the investigation was not disclosed, but sources close to the bank speculated it stems from bond losses "reported at more than $1 million" during the first nine months of 1973.
>
> It was learned last night that UP filed claims last August attempting to collect $1.2 million from its bonding company or insuror for losses supposedly caused by two former employees.
>
> UP president William M. Matthews would not identify the employees named in the civil claims, but said copies of all such claims 'must be filed with the U.S. Attorney's office when a bank is involved.'
>
> At least seven executives or former executives of Union Planters have been issued subpoenas requiring them to testify before the Grand Jury during its current session.[183]

Nine days later the public got an inkling that Union Planters might have trouble collecting more than $10,000,000 which had been loaned to Stax Records and its subsidiaries. This possibility was revealed when Memphis newspapers reported a $10,500,000 lawsuit filed in Chancery Court by Union Planters National Bank against CBS, Inc.; Stax; and officers of Stax. The lawsuit alleged that CBS had unlawfully gained control of Stax through an agreement which gave CBS exclusive nationwide distribution rights for Stax Records. Upon signing the agreement, Stax had received approximately $6,000,000 which it used to redeem 50% of its capital stock. Union Planters alleged that this was an unlawful use of the funds because it harmed other Stax creditors by "depleting the net working capital and net worth of Stax. UP was 'deceived as to the purpose for which the proceeds advanced by CBS were used or intended to be used' and the Memphis bank agreed to loan Stax more money after being told the $6 million would be used for 'operational purposes only,' the suit said."[184]

The Comptroller of the Currency asked to meet with Union Planters' entire board of directors on November 22, 1974, to discuss issuing a cease and desist order against the bank. Such an order publicly requires a bank's directors and management to cease engaging in illegal and/or unsound banking practices. Needless to say, the Comptroller's office received the board's full attention. Issuance of a cease and desist order would have been disastrous for Union Planters, for it probably would have resulted in losing its large corporate deposit base. Such a loss of financial resources most likely would have resulted in the bank becoming insolvent, having to close, and possibly causing large personal liability for the members of the board. The board hired attorneys in Washington, D.C., who were successful in forestalling the order. Matthews also wrote a letter to the Comptroller of the Currency outlining why a cease and desist order was both unnecessary and counter-productive. The Comptroller's office responded by stating, in effect, that it did not believe Union Planters would make it, but would give Matthews a chance.

Although the public never learned of the potentially devastating action proposed by the Comptroller's office, the seriousness of Union Planters' situation became obvious to the investment community when Union Planters announced that it was omitting its 1974 fourth quarter dividend. On December 12, 1974, the *Wall Street Journal* published an article which stated:

> Union Planters Corp., parent of Union Planters Bank, omitted a quarterly cash dividend on its com-

mon, comprising the first such omission since 1928, the company said.

William M. Matthews, Jr., chairman of both the parent and the bank, said the fourth quarter dividend was omitted "to maintain the bank's capital position, which had been reduced as of Sept. 30 to $65 million by previously reported losses totaling $11.9 million." Union Planters this year paid three quarterly dividends of 23 cents each.[185]

On that same day, Memphis' morning newspaper, *The Commercial Appeal*, reported that a Federal Grand Jury was renewing its inquiry into activities at Union Planters National Bank.[186] To counter reports that Union Planters' general operations were being probed, Matthews issued a memo to bank employees which also was delivered to Memphis' evening newspaper, *The Memphis Press-Scimitar*. The memo stated:

> Management feels compelled to respond to clear up any false conclusions that might result.
>
> The Grand Jury investigation which prompted this action results from complaints filed with the Justice Department by bank management. I want to assure you that to our knowledge the current complaints involve former employees and [are] not directed either against our bank or current employees.[187]

Elsewhere in the memo, Matthews stated that the actions being investigated occurred "months ago and are hopefully behind us."[188] The next day, both Memphis newspapers reported that the Federal Grand Jury had returned separate indictments against two former Union Planters' employees on charges that they had embezzled more than $286,000 from Union Planters Bank.[189]

Late in December of 1974, Union Planters' management learned of other massive losses through employee infidelity, this time in the commercial loan area and involving the bank's former senior lending officer and another experienced commercial loan officer; the problems included misapplication of bank funds, receiving things of value in return for credit approvals, and making false entries in certain bank records.

As 1974 drew to a close, Matthews faced a multitude of problems, all of which had to be overcome in order for the bank to survive. These problems were: (1) inadequate bank capital; (2) lack of controls (which was readily being solved); (3) personnel problems from changing management philosophy; (4) numerous large problem loans; (5) dishonest employees; (6) pressure from the Comptroller of the Currency; and (7) adverse reactions of the Memphis public. If the bank was to survive, Matthews had to: (1) obtain adequate capital; (2) keep the billion dollar bank's doors open and appease customers to gain the time necessary to solve the bank's many serious problems; (3) attract personnel Matthews could trust; (4) establish policies and effect controls to forestall new problems while he was trying to solve existing problems; (5) develop solutions to individual problem loans; (6) keep both bank regulators and stockholders informed; (7) keep employee morale up; and (8) develop satisfactory solutions to the bank's problems while trying (if possible) to strengthen Union Planters' position in the Memphis market.

Each of those problems was critical. However, two were especially important. Matthews had to convince the Comptroller of the Currency that he was not part of the problem but part of the solution. He also had to obtain an independent audit and publish the bank's annual report as quickly as possible in order to convince both the public and the much-needed corporate depositors of Union Planters that the bank was totally aware of its financial position and was working successfully to improve it.

During December, Matthews and Trippeer went to Washington, D.C., to meet with representatives of the Comptroller of the Currency. The bank's overriding problem was its liquidity. The Comptroller's office recognized this problem as a common one: many banks throughout the United States were beginning to evidence liquidity problems as a result of previous aggressive loan strategies. One subject in serious dispute, which was discussed thoroughly during the meeting, was Matthews' theory of proper accounting practices. Generally Accepted Accounting Principles applied outside of the banking industry held that an asset did not have to be charged off immediately merely because it was reserved against. The Comptroller's office felt, however, that reserved loans must be charged off as soon as possible. When the Comptroller's ultra-conservative method was used, a bank often ended up collecting as much as 40% of the amounts charged off—many borrowers often were able to refinance at another bank and pay off at least part of their charged off loan. Matthews and Trippeer convinced the Comptroller's office that automatic chargeoffs were theoretically unsound and dangerously unwise during a period when so many banks across the United States were in trouble and loanable funds were in extremely short supply.

By the time they left the meeting, Matthews and Trippeer had gained much needed credibility with the Comptroller's office—and much needed time for Union Planters National Bank. They were able to keep Union Planters' doors open during a financial crisis equal to the Panic of 1907, the Panic of 1914, and the Great Depression. However, simply keeping the bank's doors open was merely a first and very temporary step. To remain open, Union Planters promptly had to conceive and implement a successful turn-around strategy. Matthews had promised to effect a turn-around when he came to Union Planters. Despite the many surprises and the almost overwhelming seriousness of the bank's numerous problems, Matthews now had to deliver—and quickly.

Capital is the life's blood of a banking institution; it is the product which the firm buys and sells. At year-end 1974, Union Planters Corporation and its subsidiaries reported a net loss of $16,753,220. Capital was reduced by $18,800,000 during the year, from $78,500,000 to $59,700,000. And $10,000,000 of the capital which remained was a highly controversial asset, recorded on the balance sheet as "bond claims receivable." (The asset represented a conservative estimate of the minimum amount the bank expected to recover from its fidelity bonding companies because of insured leases incurred through the dishonesty of former officers and employees.) As of December 31, 1973, the bank's ratio of equity capital to total assets was only 5.98%; for similar banks, (those with average assets below $2 billion), the ratio was 6.58%. After the asset structure of the bank shrank by $187,000,000 during 1974, Union Planters' capital to total assets ratio declined to 5.31%, while the ratio for similar banks fell hardly at all (to 6.45%).[190]

Union Planters had an extremely large amount of loans which were not accruing interest, in addition to other non-earning assets, which put it in a vulnerable position. Matthews had to make certain that the bank's capital position did not fall below $52,000,000 because that would have resulted in legal insolvency. Although government regulators most likely would have given the bank 30 days in which to solve the capital deficiency, all the news being reported about the bank made it unlikely that additional capital could have been raised. In order for the bank to survive, management had to hold operating expenses in line at a time when it had to incur the extraordinary expense of developing work-out solutions to numerous problem loans. Adequate controls had to be established, personnel had to be reduced, and the bank had to rely increasingly on automation.

Because Union Planters was unable to obtain additional funds in the capital market, two other means of ensuring that the bank's capital remained adequate were devised: (1) decrease the bank's assets and increase leverage; and (2), through proper tax planning, create a loss carryback that would allow the bank to recoup federal taxes paid in prior years. Union Planters' situation also demanded the prompt implementation of innovative and effective strategies dealing with public relations and marketing, in addition to its capital-strengthening strategy. To a great extent, Matthews' ability quickly to conceive, design, and implement these three strategies and to make each mesh with the others, thereby enhancing their effectiveness, was the key to the salvation of Union Planters.

Having gained time with the Comptroller, the bank also had to gain time with the public until the turnaround could take effect. That required successful public relations and marketing strategies which would cost money to fund. Public confidence in the bank had to be maintained during this crisis—and maintained in the face of continued adverse publicity. The Special Loans Department of the bank was moving as swiftly as possible to solve the more than $60,000,000 worth of problem loans, protect the bank's collateral, and generate as much cash as quickly as possible. This not only involved private work-out agreements, but also publicized foreclosures, resales of foreclosed properties, and deficiency judgment lawsuits. All these activities required the bank to incur large consulting and legal fees. The bank was sued and counter-sued by many borrowers who were unwilling or unable to meet their obligations. Many borrowers went into bankruptcy. At times it seemed almost as if the entire resources of the bank were being absorbed by the massive amount of litigation in which it was embroiled.

Many of the bank's activities were reported by the local and national news media, fostering constant rumors about Union Planters' solvency, liquidity, and viability. The publicity fires were constantly being refueled, particularly by the long sequence of indictments and subsequent criminal trials of former Union Planters employees and customers. Every reduction in personnel or other cut-back in the bank's operations, every announced business decision, and especially Union Planters' quarterly financial figures were also closely monitored by the news media and by the Comptroller's office. Maintaining confidence in the bank was essential. That confidence was continually threatened by publicity. However, if positive operating results could be generated, much of the otherwise unwanted publicity might begin to have a positive effect.

Matthews' public relations strategy ultimately depended on the success of the turn-around as much as the turn-around depended on maintaining confidence. This interrelationship can be seen with particular clarity in connection with Matthews' handling of employee morale. As might be expected, suspicion, distrust, and fear became rampant among employees, particularly as well-liked and trusted senior officers were indicted. Personnel changes were necessarily frequent, and many employees began to lose confidence in their positions, in each other, and in the future of the bank. Matthews continually expressed confidence in the bank's staff and optimism about the turn-around. He quickly adopted a policy of immediately informing the entire bank of each adverse development so that employees heard of them first from management before reading about them in the newspapers. All employees were enlisted in the effort to work diligently to accomplish the turn-around. As a result, employee loyalty and dedication improved dramatically, and the bank's staff was eager and able to focus full attention on the task of turning a profit with maximum confidence and minimum distractions.

In January of 1975, a timely article appeared in the *Press-Scimitar* which accurately portrayed Matthews as an extremely hard-worker laboring successfully to solve the bank's problems. The article, entitled "UP Board Chairman Shuns Role of Social Leader," began with a discussion of one of Matthews' controversial remarks. He had been quoted as saying he would never join a country club in Memphis. "What I really said was that I don't think that I could make any money at a country club," Matthews explained in the interview. The article then stated that what Matthews actually had said was, "I haven't been able to join such groups because I have been too busy attempting to solve the problems facing our bank." The article went on to point out that Matthews: regularly put in a twelve-hour day at the bank; had been described by some observers as the smartest financial man in the Southeast; had made several tough decisions, including the firing of personnel, turning in dishonest employees, and omitting the bank's dividend; and was extremely interested in the growth and development of Memphis, Tennessee.[191]

Also in January of 1975, *The Commercial Appeal* published an article entitled "Matthews' Decision-Making Ability is Chief Asset." The article discussed the bank's problems, described how Matthews had retained complete responsibility for major decisions because of the seriousness of the bank's problems, and told how Matthews was attempting to create an organization in which other top management personnel could begin making decisions. The last two paragraphs of the article stated:

> All this boils down to Matthews' biggest problem—
> "retaining public confidence." Despite the fact that
> Union Planters' most serious problems are now be-
> hind it, and the bank is fundamentally sound, all the
> bad publicity has taken its toll.
> "What I am trying to do is cleanse the image of the
> bank," Matthews said. "We'll have to stick to our
> knitting."[192]

Matthews practiced his public relations strategy on
Union Planters' stockholders just as he did with other
groups. His letter to shareholders in the 1974 Annual
Report revealed that the corporation had sustained a net
loss for 1974 of $16,753,200 or $5.46 per share, compared with earnings of $.93 per share in 1973. But he
went on to state that the bank had employed competent
new officers who were assisting him in solving the bank's
problems. He predicted that unfavorable economic conditions would probably continue in Memphis, and he
explained that it was necessary to omit the fourth quarter
dividend in order to rebuild the corporation's capital
base which had been eroded by large losses. Matthews
personally assured the shareholders that the entire management team would "continue to exert every effort to
resolve the problems which remain ahead."[193]

Praised for its open, frank approach with the media,
Union Planters was lauded in a periodical published by
the editorial staff of *Bankers Magazine* and distributed to
leaders of banks throughout the country. The article,
entitled "How to Deal with Bad News Constructively a 'la
Union Planters," stated:

> When a bank gets into difficult situations, its man-
> agement's time and efforts should be devoted exclu-
> sively to working out solutions to the problems at
> hand. Unfortunately, however, a good deal of senior

officer attention must be diverted to the task of coping with the public relations aspects of the problem.

Media relations have been a sore spot with bankers for the past year. And the bigger the bank, the bigger the problems, the more intensive and widespread the news coverage.

The failures of U.S. National Bank, San Diego, and Franklin National Bank, New York, demonstrated the vulnerability of the industry to rumor and bad news as practically every bank in the country found at least some of its customers were wondering about the safety of their funds.

In these circumstances, a lesson can be learned from the management at Union Planters Corp., Memphis, which has had a series of shocks that are the equivalent of anything that has hit elsewhere in the system, coupled with what appears to be a number of instances where former officers and employees engaged in illegal transactions.

While few bankers would really want to have to emulate the experience of the $900 million bank, the approach that has been used probably is worth thinking about, whatever the scale of a bank's difficulties . . .

Throughout its period of turmoil, the Memphis bank has been willing to discuss its problems with the press, rather than avoiding statements or issuing bland, unrealistic announcements suggesting that everything is rosy.

Although the accessibility of the Union Planters' management and its willingness to talk intelligently about its problems has not kept the bad news out of the papers, it probably has had the effect of reducing the amount of misinformation and speculation that would have resulted if the bank hid behind the old "no comments" approach. And, as bad as the news might be, it can never be as tough as the rumors that will spring up when the community is afraid that the facts are being withheld.

Union Planters' openness has probably gotten more

favorable information into the press coverage than might otherwise have been the case. Certainly, the general press would not simply [sic] rumors that can be disspelled—is to lay its cards on the table and treat its customers as intelligent individuals who will make sound judgments when properly informed.[194]

Matthews' strategy proved very effective as litigation mounted during 1975. The bank filed suits against problem loan borrowers and ex-employees during 1975 seeking to recover slightly more than $40,000,000. Problem loan borrowers and ex-employees in turn sued the bank for more than $141,000,000 that year, a sum more than double the amount of the bank's stockholders' equity as the year began. Also, both local and national news media regularly reported the steady stream of indictments, guilty pleas, criminal trials, convictions, and jail sentences of former officers and customers.

Public relations, organizations, and other strategies were often intermeshed. A good example is presented by the litigation management techniques implemented by Matthews. In February of 1975, Matthews asked James A. Cook, Jr., to organize a special support unit responsible for major litigation, called Financial Affairs. Cook was an experienced certified public accountant who had come to the bank two and a half years earlier and had been serving as chief financial officer. His initial task was to pursue the $16,500,000 in fidelity bond claims which the bank filed. Before the end of 1975, Financial Affairs employed 14 persons and was also managing most of the bank's other major litigation, involving a total of approximately $1/4 *billion*. Cook's unit tightly controlled the litigation, kept track of deadlines, pushed the lawyers to meet them, monitored expenses, and performed many support functions for the bank officers and the lawyers involved in the lawsuits. The unit kept complete files, wrote analyses and reports, and obtained and retrieved information when it was needed. In short, it operated an information management and retrieval system for use in litigation.

Financial Affairs' existence and performance provided a number of major benefits. Legal expenses were minimized because lawyers did not have to spend time or spin wheels on a roomful of documents. The bank was able to operate more efficiently because other officers were largely relieved of such constant and time-consuming tasks as responding to inquiries, obtaining information, and locating documents for litigation. The litigation proceeded more efficiently because Financial Affairs was able to provide information quickly as needed. During this period the bank was inundated by subpoenas for bank documents from the U. S. Attorney's office and from criminal defendants. Financial Affairs quickly developed a professional working relationship with the former, and was able to avoid overbroad and burdensome subpoenas asking for every document in existence because the prosecutors knew the bank could and would promptly supply necessary information. Deliberately burdensome subpoenas from criminal defendants were usually limited by judges because of the bank's professional response to legitimate requests. Discovery requests in civil cases were handled similarly—and with similar results.

Financial Affairs also was a strategic weapon of some significance. On occasion, when strategy dictated, Cook's unit responded fully to outrageously overbroad and burdensome requests for information (usually filed to achieve delay). Such responses astonished and confused the opposition, and helped convince bench, bar, litigants, and others that Union Planters was deadly serious, and formidably so.

Thus, Financial Affairs: (1) minimized the bank's

operating expenses; (2) maximized operational and litigation efficiency; (3) ultimately contributed materially to solving the capital deficiency problem; (4) contributed to employee morale; and (5) enhanced the bank's image as a soundly-functioning, although troubled, institution. And it did so while performing a task at the focal point of the steady stream of unfavorable publicity and ugly rumors which persisted. Almost uniquely, Financial Affairs was the embodiment of the sort of innovation, reorganization, control, balance sheet management, dedication, and public relations which Matthews was using to preserve Union Planters and to solve its problems.

Union Planters also continued to fill newspapers and magazines with *positive* news about its reorganization and its innovative strategies and techniques. On February 21, William Dick became senior lending officer. A newspaper article (entitled "Bank Trims Staff to Cut Costs") pointed out that Union Planters had reduced its staff by 180 persons to 1665 employees.[195] On July 1 *The Commercial Appeal* reported the elevation of four young officers, who became executive vice presidents, and the selection of another Georgia bank executive, Quincy McPherson, to the vice-chairmanship of the Union Planters Corporation.[196]

The crime wave that had hit Union Planters, the results of which were still being reported by media throughout the country, was itself turned into a positive note in an article appearing in the October 27 issue of *Business Week*. The article analyzed the causes, costs, and solutions to the employee-infidelity problem which had existed at Union Planters:

> At the root of Union Planters' problems, Matthews believes, was an incredible lack of corporate control, coupled with low pay scales that he feels encouraged dishonesty. Matthews moved quickly to solve both problems. In January there was a hefty across-the-

board increase, given on the theory that adequately paid personnel would be less inclined to steal. And the new controls, while perhaps not unique among banks, were stringent by Union Planters' standards. Before Matthews came, any loan officer could commit the bank to its legal limit of $7.5 million to a borrower. Now limits have been clamped on loan officers, and Matthews has installed a monitoring system that he says will not only keep risky loans off the books but will also detect corruption quickly.

The rampant dishonesty at Union Planters has already been costly, though. The bank's big deficit last year primarily reflected $27.7 million in loan losses, of which $10 million is directly attributable to criminal activity, according to the bank. The result has been a substantial deterioration in Union Planters' capital base. Shareholders' equity shrank from $78 million to $59 million, which forced the bank to pass its dividend in each of the last three quarters. Matthews concedes that much of the bank's loss was due merely to incompetence, which could not be papered over when money became tight last year and Union Planters' overexposure in the real estate market became suddenly obvious. But white-collar crime was apparently as commonplace as poor judgment.[197]

The article quoted Jessie A. Barr, former executive vice president and senior lending officer who had resigned from Union Planters early in the year. He praised Matthews for his move to increase employees' salaries: "I had some officers under me who were responsible for $40 million in loans and they were making $12,000 and $13,000. And ninety-five percent of the loans were already made before they ever got before the loan committee."[198] The article continued:

But it is through organizational changes that Matthews is trying to avoid future trouble. Under the old system, nearly all the bank's business was under the jurisdiction of two executive vice-presidents. Now there are six and, although they report to Trippeer, they have direct access to Matthews as well. Matthews thinks the system will eliminate bottlenecks of the past and allow problems to come to his attention quickly.

. . . Adopting a system used by most medium-sized and large banks, he also set up three committees either to approve loans beforehand or to review them, depending on their size.

One loan committee, which must have at least three outside directors as members, reviews all loans of $1 million or more and checks the entire loan portfolio quarterly . . . .

Matthews believes that if his routine controls had been in effect all along, the loan losses—and the criminal activity—could have been cut substantially. Trippeer seems to agree. "If someone really wants to get you," he says, "he is going to do it. But Matthews' philosophy is not to make it easy for him."[199]

By this time, the vast majority of the continuing publicity about Union Planters was favorable, and the periodic surprises were happy ones. Indeed, the turnaround appeared all the more dramatic because of Matthews' full disclosure policy. Thus, a policy born out of short-term necessity proved to have considerable longer-term benefits as well.

Because of its precarious financial position, the bank had to reduce overhead dramatically. The closing of unprofitable branches required the development and implementation of a marketing strategy for offering numerous services at minimum cost. Periodic announcements and previews of coming attractions were made to reinforce the public's confidence that the bank was sound and moving forward. The acceptability in the market place of these innovative services was critically important, because Union Planters could ill afford to lose any of its existing market share to its competitors.

During 1975, Union Planters bombarded the public with new marketing programs and services. These included a $100 rebate offer on all new automobile installment loans, later expanded to include home improvement loans as well (of $2000 or more). The bank also installed a new service, called Telechecking, which enabled customers to transfer funds from savings accounts to checking accounts simply by calling a special number at Union Planters. In June 1975, Union Planters announced that it would install 30 automatic teller machines in Memphis and Shelby County within the next two years. These facilities would be open 24 hours a day and permit customers to transfer funds between accounts, make installment payments, obtain cash advances on MasterCharge cards, withdraw funds, and make deposits at any time of day or night. Later that month, Union Planters also announced that it would add tax sheltered individual retirement accounts to the numerous other services it offered its customers.

One month later, the bank announced that it would begin offering bank credit cards in the name of both husband and wife upon request. Both parties would share the credit responsibility, but each would have separate credit information entered on his record. Union Planters also announced in July the first stage of an electronic payroll deposit system through which Social Security recipients could have their payments sent directly to Union Planters and deposited automatically in their accounts.

On September 1, 1975, Union Planters began sending its customers a Union Planters Services card for use in its 24-hour automatic teller machines. Union Planters' management stated that these machines were able to handle 90% of routine customer transactions, around the clock, every day of the week. Matthews and Rawlins had built a similar system at the First National Bank of

Annie, Union Planters Anytime Teller.

Atlanta. Considerable creative thought, time, and effort were devoted to personalizing and de-mystifying the machine. Union Planters' ads showed a wholesome, All-American girl easily using the machine, which the bank named "Annie, the Anytime Teller." Management felt that if it could get a customer to utilize the machine three times, the customer would begin utilizing the service on a regular basis. The program was an instant and continuing success, the number of transactions far exceeding projections at every stage of implementation.

The bank also added services by diversifying into

bank-related areas in 1975. Union Planters National Leasing, Inc., was organized to lease all types of equipment and to assist correspondent banks either by helping them set up their own leasing departments or by participating in certain lease agreements with them. Madison Loan and Thrift Company was formed to collect certain charged off loans of the bank. Automated Financial Systems, Inc., was established to provide "comprehensive technical assistance for the installation and use of certain data processing programs designed to enable small and medium-sized banks to process their daily work on relatively inexpensive computer hardware."[200]

Also in 1975, Union Planters closed its Bellevue branch, which had consistently lost money since it opened in 1965. Management's marketing strategy—offering numerous services at minimum cost, primarily using electronic funds transfers—meant that several other branches would soon close as well.

In November of 1975, the bank introduced a valuable new service for large accounts. It offered certificates of deposit of $100,000 or more, with maturities of between six and 18 months, which earned interest at a fluctuating rate tied to Union Planters' prime rate. These certificates kept large deposits in the bank by permitting the depositor to take advantage of the higher interest rates paid on longer-maturing certificates and also to receive the benefit of rising interest rates.

In December of 1975, Union Planters announced it was expanding its "Annie" services to include Memphians whose checking accounts were at other banks. Such customers were charged a fee of one dollar for processing the application and issuing an "Annie" card, and a service fee of $.25 per transaction for processing through the customer's bank. Holders of the "Annie" card also were permitted to cash checks for up to $25.00 at any Union Planters' branch.

In 1976 management reorganized the bank into four areas to simplify and coordinate the bank's marketing and operations functions. A Commercial Group was formed to include the Agricultural, National, Metropolitan, Investment, International, Real Estate, and Marketing divisions. The Greater Memphis Group was composed of the Automation, Operations, Retail, and Consumer Lending divisions. The Trust Division continued to be separate. The Staff Group, consisting of the Personnel, Loan Administration, and Financial division, provided administrative and support services for the bank.

Union Planters continued to inundate the public with numerous new services in 1976. In February it announced that the First National Bank of West Memphis had become the first bank in the Mid-South to purchase the "Annie" automatic teller system. On May 14, Union Planters announced the closing of three inner-city branches which had had little or no growth in volume or number of accounts, explaining that the bank preferred to apply its resources to areas in which there was greater potential for growth.

On May 27, Union Planters announced that within the next 30 days it would be offering shoppers an alternative to checkwriting. By using Union Planters Services card at the point of sale, the cost of a purchase would be deducted directly from the customer's checking account. More than 100 merchants signed up for the program before the announcement, and the bank stated that it expected between 300 and 400 additional merchants to join within 30 days. As an initial inducement to use the service card, Union Planters offered a two percent rebate on all purchases during the first several weeks of the program. The program, known as UPShopping, began on June 11.

On June 1, management announced that five additional "Annie" automatic tellers would be opened in Shelby County during the year. The five locations (Whitehaven, Bartlett, Frayser, Germantown and Laurelwood) were selected because the majority of the residents in these areas were relatively young and could adapt faster to the new equipment and modern technology. Quincy McPherson, executive vice president and head of the Commercial Group at Union Planters, announced on June 20 that the bank was offering merchant banking services. Merchant banking was a group of financial services slowly being adopted by many of the nation's largest banks. Rather than merely accepting deposits and lending short-term money, merchant bankers arranged for non-bank financing for a fee, offered financial advice to customers, made longer-term loans, and assisted with mergers and acquisitions.

On June 27, Union Planters announced another new concept for Memphis retail banking. It eliminated the all too familiar teller line at its Mendenhall branch and replaced it with tellers sitting at desks near three "Annie" machines. Routine banking functions, such as cashing checks and making deposits, were to be handled primarily by "Annie." "Our sit-down tellers, in addition to their usual responsibilities of accepting deposits and cashing checks, will open savings and checking accounts, issue Cashier and Travelers checks, and eventually accept installment loan applications and perform other banking services not usually associated with a teller."[201] On June 28, Union Planters announced its "60-plus plan" card. This program allowed persons aged 60 and older to receive discounts of up to 25% on services and merchandise at selected stores.

Union Planters continued to expand its "Annie" program and announced on September 19 that automated teller machines would be placed in 30 grocery and retail stores within the next 60 days:

Extension of the service will in effect make it possible for UP customers not only to pay for merchandise or obtain cash by electronic transfer of money from their savings or checking accounts, but also to make a deposit and receive immediate credit in their account for the deposit.

The system will begin operating in Giant and Pic-Pac food stores in mid-October, and will be expanded to other locations within 30 to 60 days after introduction . . . .

In a typical grocery, or retail store transaction, [Rawlins] said, a customer will select his purchases in the normal way and take them to the checkout area, where automated terminals will be located.

The shopper will place a purchase draft (similar to a charge card receipt) in the Annie terminal, and will use his UPS card (a charge-like, plastic card) to have the funds electronically transferred to the merchant's account. He then will present the coded draft to the clerk at the checkout register, where it will be treated like cash.

"The expansion of the Annie program into high-volume retail stores, such as groceries, will complete the electronic point-of-sale network the city needs to offer both convenient checking and savings account access in retail stores to bank customers, and protection from check losses for any particular merchant," Rawlins said.

"These installations [will] bring to fifty-four the number of "Annie" locations in Memphis."[202]

On October 8, Union Planters announced the installation of a new "UPS Balance Line" in seven branches in order to determine whether it should install the system in all Union Planters' branches. The balance line system would allow customers to determine their checking and savings account balances by using their Union Planters Service card and a special machine located in the branch's lobby.

On October 13, 1976, *The Commercial Appeal* reported that "Union Planters National Bank has become the first major bank in the Nation to establish a comingled option fund for pension and profit-sharing accounts."[203] Four days later, Union Planters announced in *The Commercial Appeal* that it planned to add to its services by honoring BankAmericard deposits from local merchants in addition to its long-standing MasterCharge operation.[204]

In addition to the bank's efforts on its own behalf to become an innovative and profitable financial institution, Union Planters also attempted to improve Memphis during 1976. It funded the Memphis Development Foundation, a not-for-profit organization formed initially to develop a commercial center by renovating three warehouses on the bluffs overlooking the Mississippi River. Management believed that this development, named Beale Street Landing, would play a pivotal role in the redevelopment of downtown Memphis.

As the multitude of problems which had plagued Union Planters since 1974 began to ameliorate, Matthews increasingly turned his attention to the many problems faced by Memphis, because he strongly felt that a bank cannot grow faster than the community in which it is located. During 1976, he proposed that an independent, outside, unbiased group conduct a study to determine the direction of Memphis' future. In a speech to the Mid-South Association of Business Economists, he said:

> While the rest of the country is recovering from recession, "Memphis is hobbling along like a crippled giant." . . . We seem to lack dynamics or an understanding of which direction we should grow . . . . Memphis has a great heritage and a great economic foundation from which to grow. Unfortunately, it also has a tendency to look to that past for its future.
> Looking at the past to improve upon the city's agricultural and distribution experience is fine. But, he

said, the city also must look to new ways to expand its distribution system in order to compete in national markets.

He proposed, "that the business and political leadership [in the City] come together to raise sufficient funds to undertake an intensive and extensive development plan produced by parties outside of the City with no vested interests to determine the optimum direction of growth for the City."[205]

Union Planters also continued to develop new services in 1977, and announced a program that allowed customers with 36-month installment loans to skip up to three payments per year, if prearranged with and approved by the bank's management. Thus the program made it possible to stretch a 36-month loan over 48 months with bank approval. On June 3, 1977, Union Planters Leasing, Inc. announced plans to offer leveraged lease financing for the first time. Five days later, Union Planters announced a further advance in its strategy of providing a variety of services at minimum cost through electronic funds transfers. As of September 1, customers could pay their bills by telephone. In a newspaper article, Ben Rawlins praised the future service: "[T]he real aim of telephone checking is to attract depositors .... [T]he bank's aggressive marketing is 'having an impact' on retail and demand deposits. They are significantly up and we think they will continue going up."[206]

On June 19, 1977, Union Planters' Real Estate and Mortgage Loan Department announced plans to solicit first mortgage loans. Due to continuing low commercial loan demand in Memphis, mortgage loans of 10 to 30 years with a minimum loan amount of $25,000 would be sought. On September 16, 1977, Union Planters announced that Visa credit cards would be added to the line of credit cards being offered by the bank. On

September 19, the bank announced that it had formed a new subsidiary, Chickasaw Capital Corporation, the first licensed MESBIC (Minority Enterprise Small Business Investment Corporation) in Memphis. MESBIC operated under a Small Business Administration program designed to help economically disadvantaged Americans, including Vietnam War veterans and members of minority races, obtain business financing otherwise unavailable to them.

Fighting for its existence at the end of 1974, Union Planters had to change its capital strategy if a turnaround was to be achieved. The bank had to: (1) continue to maintain and improve its capital base; (2) set up credit lines around the country to hold deposits (utilizing high cost federal funds as a last resort); (3) eliminate problem loans as quickly as possible, and (4) generate earnings on its assets. Innovative tax planning also was necessary to allow earnings to remain in the bank, thereby increasing its capital position.

Prompt preparation and dissemination of Union Planters' financial data, particularly the *1974 Annual Report*, was extremely critical to maintaining public confidence. Just as the bank's original management in 1874 had openly discussed the ousting of its first president, William M. Farrington, Matthews openly discussed the bank's problems with the press, depositors, borrowers, and stockholders. Confidence was restored and maintained by directly answering all questions in an open and truthful manner instead of trying to avoid and evade the issues.

On March 7, 1975, Union Planters' published what was probably the most important *Annual Report* in its history. In his letter to the shareholders, Matthews stated: "The most significant factor affecting the corporation's results of operations for 1974 was the $25.6 million provision made for loan losses. By comparison, a

$7.0 million provision for loan losses was charged against earnings in 1973." Assuring stockholders that loan loss reserves were adequate, Matthews pointed out that large loan losses had been caused by the adverse effect of general economic conditions on the bank's borrowing customers, by inflation, and by the "misconduct, dishonesty and infidelity of certain former employees of the bank."[207] He also noted that the bank had filed claims aggregating $16,500,000 with its bonding company to recover losses incurred through the misconduct, dishonesty and infidelity of former employees. Certain that it would receive at least $10,000,000 from the bonding company, the bank listed an unusual item called "bond claims receivable" as an asset on the balance sheet.[208] The effect of adding this asset was to reduce losses due to loan charge offs by $10,000,000. This then-novel asset was vital to the bank's solvency.

Another reason for the loss incurred in 1974 was a decrease in the bank's net interest margin due to the high cost of short-term money, which the bank was having to obtain in the national money markets. Matthews confidently stated that the net interest margin problem was readily being solved by rationing credit and reducing loan levels.[209]

As a result of 1974 operations, the total assets of Union Planters Corporation and its subsidiaries declined by approximately $187,000,000 to $1.124 billion, retained earnings declined by $15,400,000 to $10,058,350, and shareholders' equity declined by approximately $18,800,000 to $59,652,746. The price of Union Planters' stock declined in 1974 from a high in the first quarter of $21.50 bid-$22.50 asked, to a low of $6.25 bid-$7.25 asked in the fourth quarter.[210] Nevertheless, the bank remained viable, and management was successfully pursuing carefully designed strategies dealing with the bank's public relations, marketing, and capital problems.

In reporting Union Planters' operating results for 1975, Matthews pointed out in his letter to stockholders that the firm in 1975 had sustained a net loss of $2,750,149, or $.90 per share as compared with a net loss in 1974 of $16,753,220, or $5.46 per share. Although the Corporation continued to operate at a loss, its position was improving dramatically. The improvement was due to a much smaller provision for losses on loans and fore-closed properties, which was $11,500,000 less in 1975 than a year earlier. The bank's non-earning assets (loans on non-accrual and total foreclosed assets) continued to be a problem. Although loans on non-accrual decreased by $13,600,000 to $48,400,000, total foreclosed assets increased during 1975 from $8,800,000 to $35,700,000 as a result of management's decision to work the problem loans aggressively. But management was able to convert approximately $11,000,000 of foreclosed properties into revenue-earning assets during the year.[211] As had been projected in the *1974 Annual Report*, management was able to improve Union Planters' liquidity position by maintaining a stable deposit base and significantly reducing the amount of funds purchased in the money market. Liquidity was also improved by selling a portion of the assets of the bank's Galbreath subsidiary.

Matthews continued to work on a tax strategy, ulti-mately devising a daring plan which began to operate in 1975. A 1969 federal tax law had given banks the right to recapture up to 10 years of prior taxes paid, but only to the extent of losses incurred after 1975. Union Planters stood to gain $9,600,000 if the law could be used. The difficult strategic problem was to find a way to structure a maximum tax loss in 1976 without interrupting the turn-around. Union Planters achieved this objective by using its securities investment account to accelerate income in accordance with legal opinions obtained from Washing-ton tax counsel, and the bank actually paid a small amount of taxes in 1975. Those taxes were paid although the bank had reported substantial losses for the previous two years. Acceleration of taxable income into 1975 resulted in a substantial increase in tax losses for 1976. Thus at year-end 1976, Union Planters qualified to claim a refund of taxes paid during the preceding 10 years.

The total assets of Union Planters Corporation and its subsidiaries fell during 1975 by $135,800,000, to $988,364,295. The net operating loss for the year, along with management's decision in the fourth quarter to issue a cash dividend of $.20 per share, reduced the bank's retained earnings to $8,644,074, a reduction of $1,400,000 for the year. Stockholders' equity declined by $3,300,000 to $56,288,470.[212]

Although the bank's marketing strategy was receiving most of the publicity in local newspapers, the Special Loans Department continued working diligently and effectively to reduce the bank's non-earning assets. In 1976 the bank also formed a wholly-owned subsidiary, HHUP of Memphis, Inc., to complete, operate, and dispose of foreclosed real estate. Its accomplishments were illustrated in the bank's *1976 Annual Report*; non-earning assets decreased during that year by $26,700,000 to $57,400,000. The bank's loan portfolio also continued to improve; the provision for losses on loans and foreclosed assets decreased from $14,100,000 during 1975 to $10,700,000 during 1976. Management's belt-tightening policy also was continuing; Union Planters' personnel declined from 1,607 to 1,379 persons in 1976[213]

On August 10, 1976, Union Planters announced that it was buying $6,000,000 worth of second mortgage loans on single-family homes in Florida, prompted primarily by low loan demand locally in the installment loan sector of the bank: "The bank purchased in July $2.5 million in the loans, which have an average investment life of 40 months or less. The balance of the transaction is to be delivered in $500,000 increments bimonthly."[214]

Union Planters' total operating income decreased in 1976 by $8,485,171. Of that decrease, $6,164,861 was attributable to a decline in interest income. The operating loss before income taxes and security transactions was $10,129,605. But income tax credits of $6,258,333, plus a net gain on securities transactions of $3,036,818, reduced the Corporation's net loss to $834,454, or $.26 per share. Total assets increased by $20,111,249 to $1,008,475,554. The $834,454 net loss, together with a $.05 per share cash dividend declared in February and a two and a half percent stock dividend declared in May, reduced retained earnings to $7,174,338 as of December 31, 1976. Shareholders' equity declined by $902,236 during the year to $55,386,234.[215]

Union Planters' management continued devising ways to improve its capital position. In March of 1977, the bank announced that it had sold nine of its branches for $3,000,000 and had leased the branches back for 10 years with a 50-year renewal option. Also the bank that year concluded its much-publicized problems with its Stax Recording Company loans. A major step in solidifying the banks' novel $10,000,000 "bond claims receivable" occurred in June and July. On June 10, a circuit court jury returned a $4,500,000 verdict in favor of the bank in a case involving just one of the bond claims. (The verdict was appealed unsuccessfully by the bonding companies.) On July 1, Union Planters and the bonding companies agreed to settle the remaining claims for $6,300,000. In addition to restoring $6,300,000 to earnings status, the settlement was not taxable. Because Union Planters had carried the bond claims as an asset since 1974, the $6,300,000 received in 1977 was not reflected in current earnings for tax purposes. Thus the bank received $6,300,000 in tax-free income in 1977.

In its *1977 Annual Report*, Union Planters was able to celebrate a return to profitability. The company earned

$1.03 per share in 1977, compared with a loss of $.26 per share in 1976. During 1977, Union Planters was able to return approximately $37,000,000 of previously non-earning assets to an earning status primarily because non-accrual loans were reduced by $18,000,000 (to $10,000,000), the $6,300,000 received in the bond claims settlement was invested and the $4,500,000 judgment rendered in the one bond claim case which had gone to trial began accruing interest, and foreclosed assets were reduced by $8,000,000 (to $21,000,000).

The bank shifted its portfolio of investment securities to higher yielding U.S. Treasury securities; these were taxable, but, because of the bank's tax loss carry forward, the interest earned was largely tax-free for the bank. Interest on loans increased by $2,300,000, and the bank also increased direct lease financing income, fees on loans, trading account income, trust division income, and service charges on deposit accounts. Thus total operating income increased by $3,937,640 to $68,460,770 in 1977. The bank also cut total operating expenses during 1977 by $8,857,724 (to $65,795,011). Earnings on operations were $2,665,759 in 1977 (compared with a loss of $10,129,605 in 1976) before income taxes, net security transactions, and extraordinary items. Including applicable income tax credits and net profits on security transactions, net earnings for Union Planters Corporation during 1977 totalled $3,347,358, or $1.03 per share. A two and a half percent stock dividend was declared in November in order to maintain investor interest yet retain control. Retained earnings increased by $2,615,563 to $9,789,901 at year end. Stockholders' equity during the 12-month operation period also grew by $3,387,358 to $58,773,592.[216]

Thus the strategies implemented by Union Planters proved successful. Some other banks, in better financial condition than Union Planters at the end of 1974, had become insolvent and had been closed. Yet Union Planters not only continued to operate in an overbranched city with a stagnated economy, but also was able to complete a dramatic turn-around to profitability.

11
LESSONS THAT WERE LEARNED

The partial cost of employee infidelity at Union Planters Bank, net of recoveries, was approximately $48,000,000. The total cost will never be known, nor will it ever be known how many good employees did substandard jobs because of the prevailing atmosphere. It will never be known how many good prospective employees shied away from Union Planters because of the unfavorable publicity, nor will it ever be known how many business opportunities Union Planters lost because of its multitudinous problems. It is known, however, that Union Planters had a loyal group of customers who kept their accounts at the bank despite the adverse publicity and rumors, and that the bank took the proper course of action when it opted to face its problems squarely.

Analysis of the growth, the decline, the crisis, and the turn-around of Union Planters reveals several lessons to be learned. A number of these relate only to banking, but others can be applied by the management of numerous industries. A few of the more important lessons are: (1) A bank's key resources are capital and dedicated employees. Because Union Planters was able to devise methods of obtaining the necessary capital, it was able to survive. Without the perseverance and sacrifices made by its loyal employees during the bank's crisis, Union Planters would not have survived. (2) Profits, not growth, are the measure of a successful firm. Banks, like other business organizations, can over-compete to their own detriment. (3) It is imperative that the objectives of a bank, its divisions, and its departments, be thoroughly understood throughout the organization. Failure by top management to formulate and communicate clear objectives ultimately leads to disaster. (4) Employees must be paid a wage consistent with their responsibilities and duties in the firm. (5) An effective control system to maximize efficiency and insure against employee infidelity must be established. A written code of ethics for all officers, and annual compliance reports and financial statements, are necessary components of such a system. (6) It is far better to discuss a firm's problems explicitly with the news media, the investment community, employees, and stockholders than to have these groups speculate and wonder whether they are being told the whole truth. Such an approach instills confidence in management, and serves as a rumor-deterrent. (7) As is most clearly demonstrated by Union Planters' novel use of its "bond claims receivable" as an asset of the bank, top management must do what it believes is correct. Furthermore, top management must have a broad knowledge of the tax laws applicable to its field, and use them creatively. Top management must not be totally dependent on accountants, tax consultants, or lawyers. And (8) it is as important today as it was in Union Planters' early history to practice S. P. Read's philosophy: *"Eternal vigilance is the price that we must pay for our own security."*

AFTERWORD

Having accomplished the turn-around, Union Planters continues to move forward at a rapid and accelerating pace. Matthews began his letter to shareholders in the *1978 Annual Report*, by stating:

> In Union Planters Corporation's 1977 Annual Report, the letter to shareholder's noted we were entering 1978 "with a strong improvement in financial strength." This optimism proved to be well justified as net earnings for 1978 increased to $5,087,827, or $1.53 per share, from net earnings for 1977 of $3,297,825, or $.99 per share. As a result of this improvement, the Corporation's Board of Directors declared a 2½% stock dividend . . . and a five cent per share quarterly cash dividend . . . , both payable March 15, 1979. We continue to be optimistic for 1979.[217]

The Corporation reduced non-earning assets during the year by $11,000,000 to $19,900,000. Although tax loss carryforwards increased net earnings in 1978 by $1,975,000, an additional $11,200,000 in tax loss carryforwards remained available to the Corporation to shelter future income.[218]

Union Planters' *1979 Annual Report* showed continued dramatic progress. 1979 earnings (before tax credits) increased by 66.37% to $5,178,874. The Corporation was able to use a portion of its net operating loss carryforward to generate tax credits of $3,600,000, which boosted net earnings to $8,778,874. The Corporation's per share earnings in 1979 were $2.63, compared with $1.53 in 1978—a 71.9% improvement. In addition, shareholders' equity increased by $6,108,000 (9.6%) to $69,710,000, and the Board of Directors declared a quarterly dividend of 10 cents per share payable on March 14, 1980.[219] Shortly before this book went to press, bank earnings for the second quarter of 1980 were announced. A *Commercial Appeal* article stated, "Union Planters Corp. yesterday reported net income figures indicating it was the most profitable major bank in the state during the second quarter."[220]

Among the many lessons which can be learned from the way in which Union Planters successfully kept its doors open, the bank's current on-going success makes one important final lesson apparent: in dealing with a crisis, however severe and immediate, management must nevertheless prepare to deal with the future and ongoing success; a business cannot rest on its laurels; and, if it continues to apply the lessons learned through adversity, it can turn a dangerous crisis into a valuable long-term asset.

NOTES

[1]"Hard-Driving Matthews Turns Profit at Shaken Union Planters," *American Banker*, February 21, 1978.

[2]Lucille Webb Banks, "Insurance Firm Gave Memphis Bank Birth," *The Memphis Press*, March 15, 1928, from the records of the Goodwyn Institute Library.

[3]"Notice to Stockholders of DeSoto Insurance & Trust Co." (of an election to change to a bank), dated April 15, 1869, reprinted in *Souvenir of the Sixtieth Birthday of the Union Planters National Bank & Trust Co.* (1929).

[4]"The Yellow Fever Epidemics," reprinted in *Souvenir, op.cit., supra*, n. 3.

[5]"A Short History of the Union Planters National Bank & Trust Company" (an unpublished two-page document found in the bank's archives).

[6]William M. Farrington, *Address to the Stockholders of the Union & Planters Bank of Memphis* (Memphis: September 26, 1874), pp. 1-23. Insertions in parentheses by author.

[7]C. W. Goyer, et al., "To the Stockholders of the Union and Planters Bank" (October 8, 1874). (Response to Farrington's *Address to the Stockholders of the Union & Planters Bank of Memphis, op. cit., supra*), n. 6.

[8]Quoted in Union & Planters Bank & Trust Company, *The Story of a Memphis Institution: 1869-1919* (Memphis: 1919), p. 29.

[9]"The Yellow Fever Epidemics," reprinted in *Souvenir, op.cit., supra*, n. 3. Insertions in parentheses by author.

[10]*Ibid.*

[11]Lucille Webb Banks, *op.cit., supra*, n. 2.

[12]*Ibid.*

[13]*The Story of a Memphis Institution, op.cit., supra*, n. 8, p. 33.

[14]*Ibid.*, p. 10.

[15]*Ibid.*

[16]John J. Heflin (as told to a staff reporter), "Memphis Booms— Clearings Tell the Story," *The Commercial Appeal*, January 20, 1952, Section 5, p. 1.

[17]*The Story of a Memphis Institution, op.cit., supra*, n. 8, p. 12.

[18]"Union Planters National Bank: Corporate Background" (unpublished four-page report found in the bank's archives), p. 2.

[19]*Ibid.*

[20]"A Short History," *op.cit., supra*, n. 5.

[21]John Berry McFerrin, *Caldwell and Company: A Southern Financial Empire* (Vanderbilt University Press: 1969), taken from the inside front jacket cover of the book.

[22]*Ibid.*, p. 77.

[23]*Ibid.*, from the inside front jacket cover of the book and pp. 71-72.

[24]*Mid-Continent Banker* (August, 1969), p. 56.

[25]John Berry McFerrin, *op.cit., supra*, n. 21, pp. 72-77 (footnote omitted).

[26]Newspaper clipping dated November 15, 1930, from the Bank's records. Insertion in parentheses by author. Name of publisher not indicated.

[27]Newspaper clipping dated March 13, 1933, from the Bank's records. Name of publisher not indicated.

[28]Robert Talley, "Long Pillar of City, MidSouth, Historic Union Planters Bank Will Start New Era This Week," *The Commercial Appeal*, April 27, 1952, Section II, p. 5.

[29]Newspaper clipping dated April 8, 1933, from the bank's records. Name of publisher not indicated.

[30]"Alexander Advises Bankers to Drop 'Deep Blue Glasses' and Lend Money," newspaper article dated in pencil, November 8, 1934, from the bank's records. Name of publisher not indicated.

[31]*Ibid.*

[32]*Ibid.*

[33]According to newspaper clippings dated November 10, 1935, and July 7, 1936, from the Bank's records. Names of publisher not indicated.

[34]" 'Stay South,' Advises Alexander." Neither the date nor the author is listed, and it is not known whether the paper was a speech or a published article.

[35]"Union Planters National Bank: Corporate Background," *op.cit., supra*, n. 18, p. 3.

[36]*Ibid.*

[37]Memphis Chamber of Commerce, *Memphis: A Short Historical Sketch With A Summary of Important Dates* (undated), pp. 10-11.

[38]"Union Planters National Bank: Corporate Background," *op.cit., supra*, n. 18, p. 3.

[39]Taken from the Annual Reports of Union Planters National Bank & Trust Co. for the years 1942, 1943, and 1944.

[40]Union Planters National Bank & Trust Co., *77th Annual Report to Stockholders* (January 9, 1946), p. 2.

[41]*Ibid.*, pp. 4-5.

[42]*Memphis: A Short Historical Sketch, etc., op. cit., supra*, n. 37, p. 13.

[43]This information was obtained from an unpublished summary of information reported in Memphis newspapers regarding Union

Planters. A notation indicated that the news of the bank shortening its name appeared in *The Commercial Appeal* on January 15, 1952.

[44]Robert Talley, *op.cit., supra*, n. 28.

[45]Union Planters National Bank of Memphis, *84th Annual Report to Stockholders* (Memphis: January 14, 1953), pp. 2-11.

[46]Tom Meanley, "U-P's New Head Finds Phone a Busy Thing!" *The Press Scimiter*, p. 18. No date is shown on the clipping, but January 15, 1955, is presumed.

[47]*Ibid.*

[48]Union Planters National Bank of Memphis, *92nd Annual Report to Stockholders* (Memphis: January 11, 1961), pp. 2-10.

[49]*Ibid.*, p. 4.

[50]*Memphis: A Short Historical Sketch, etc., op.cit., supra*, n. 37, pp. 13 and 17.

[51]*92nd Annual Report to Stockholders, op.cit., supra*, n. 48, p. 5.

[52]Union Planters National Bank of Memphis, *93rd Annual Report to Stockholders* (Memphis: January 10, 1962), p. 3.

[53]Union Planters National Bank of Memphis, *94th Annual Report to Stockholders*, pp. 3-4.

[54]Thomas Michael, " 'Retiring' Vance Alexander Has No Plans for Leaving," *The Commerical Appeal*, January 11, 1963. No page number on clipping found in the bank's archives.

[55]*94th Annual Report to Stockholders, op.cit., supra*, n. 53, pp. 1-9.

[56]Thomas Michael, *op.cit., supra*, n. 54.

[57]Union Planters National Bank of Memphis, *95th Annual Report to Stockholders and Statement of Condition* (Memphis: January 8, 1964), pp. 1-4.

[58]Union Planters National Bank of Memphis, *96th Annual Report to Stockholders* (Memphis: January 20, 1965), pp. 1-4.

[59]*Ibid.*

[60]*Ibid.*

[61]Union Planters National Bank of Memphis, *1965 Annual Report to Stockholders*, p. 3.

[62]*Ibid.*, p. 3.

[63]*Ibid.*, pp. 6-7.

[64]*Ibid.*, pp. 2, 12.

[65]*Ibid.*, p. 2.

[66]*Ibid.*, paraphrased from p. 3.

[67]*Ibid.*, p. 3.

[68]*Ibid.*, p. 17.

[69]Union Planters National Bank of Memphis, *1966 Annual Report to Stockholders*, pp. 6-7.

[70]*Ibid.*, pp. 8-9.

[71]*Ibid.*

[72]*Ibid.*, pp. 9-10.

[73]*Ibid.*, p. 1.

[74]*Ibid.*

[75]*Ibid.*, pp. 2-3.

[76]Union Planters National Bank of Memphis, *1967 Annual Report*, p. 3.

[77]*Ibid.*, p. 2.

[78]*Ibid.*, pp. 2-3.

[79]"Retiring UP Bank Official Praised For Long Service," undated and unidentified newspaper clipping found in the bank's archives.

[80]*1967 Annual Report, op.cit., supra*, n. 76, p. 2.

[81]*Ibid*, pp. 2-3.

[82]David Pollard, "Understanding & Patience Typify New UP Board Chief," *The Commercial Appeal*, February 11, 1968, from the bank's archives; no page number on clipping.

[83]*Ibid.*

[84]*Ibid.*

[85]Union Planters National Bank of Memphis, *1968 Annual Report*, pp. 2-3.

[86]*Ibid*, p. 3.

[87]*Ibid.*, pp. 4-11.

[88]*Ibid.*

[89]Rosemary McKelvey, "Union Planters National Bank is 100 Years Old!" *Mid-Continent Banker* (August, 1969), p. 54

[90]"Branch Banking Today Part of Modern Trend of Financial Service," Memphis *Daily News*, September 12, 1969, no page number on clipping; found in bank's archives.

[91]"Young UP President Sees Gains in Year," *The Commercial Appeal*, October 11, 1970, Sec. 3, p. 10.

[92]*Finance: The Magazine of Money* (October, 1969), clipping from the bank's archives.

[93]*American Banker* (September 8, 1969), clipping from the bank's archives.

[94]Union Planters National Bank of Memphis, *1969 Annual Report*, p. 2.

[95]*Ibid.*, pp. 4-21.

[96]*Ibid.*, p. 5.

[97]*Ibid.*, pp. 5 and 18.

[98]*Ibid.*, pp. 4-21.

[99]Union Planters National Bank of Memphis, *1970 Annual Report*, p. 4.

[100]*Ibid.*, p. 19.

[101]*Ibid.*

[102]*Ibid.*, p. 16.

[103]*Ibid.*, p. 11.

[104]*Ibid.*, pp. 21-27.

[105]*Ibid.*, p. 12.

[106]*Ibid.*, p. 5.

[107]*Ibid.*, pp. 21-26.

[108]*Ibid.*, p. 5.

[109]"Bankers Expect Growth Despite Economic Conditions," *Press Scimitar*, January 13, 1971, p. D-4.

[110]*Ibid.*

[111]*Ibid.*

[112]C. Bennett Harrison, "What are the Prospects for 1971?" *Mid-Continent Banker* (January, 1971).

[113]Union Planters National Bank of Memphis, *1971 Annual Report*, p. 2.

[114]*Ibid.*, p. 18.

[115]*Ibid.*, p. 23.

[116]*Ibid.*

[117]*1970 Annual Report, op.cit., supra*, n. 99, p. 5.

[118]*Ibid.*, pp. 4, 6-20.

[119]*1971 Annual Report, op.cit., supra*, n. 113, p. 3.

[120]*Ibid.*, pp. 2, 4.

[121]*Ibid.*, pp. 6-17.

[122]McKelvey, *op.cit., supra*, n. 89.

[123]*1971 Annual Report, op.cit., supra*, n. 113, p. 2.

[124]A copy of the letter with attachments, which is now of public record, was supplied by Union Planters.

[125]*Ibid.*

[126]*Ibid.*, p. 7.

[127]*Ibid.*, pp. 7-9.

[128]*Ibid.*, pp. 9-10.

[129]*Ibid.*, p. 10.

[130]*Ibid.*, pp. 12-14.

[131]*1971 Annual Report, op.cit., supra*, n. 113, pp. 18, 19, 23.

[132]*Ibid.*, p. 19.

[133]James Cole, "Bankers Expect More Bullishness," *The Commercial Appeal*, January 9, 1972. No page number noted on clipping.

[134]"Signs Point to Growth of Mid-South Economy," *Memphis Press Scimitar*, May 4, 1972, p. 19.

[135]Louis Silver, "Banks Grow Up, Base Interest Rate on Own Area," *The Commercial Appeal*, January 13, 1972. No page number on clipping.

[136]*Ibid.*

[137]*The Wall Street Transcript*, New York, April 10, 1972. No page number on clipping.

[138]"Bank Earnings Dip," *The Commercial Appeal*, April 14, 1972. No page number on clipping.

[139]"Bank Seeks Change," *The Commercial Appeal*, May 2, 1972. No page number on clipping.

[140]Ed Dunn, "Chamber of Commerce Begins 'Believe in Memphis' Drive," *Press Scimitar*, November 21, 1972, p. 13.

[141]*Ibid.*

[142]"Remodeling Program Fosters Progressive Image," *Mid-Continent Banker* (December, 1972). No page number on clipping.

[143]Union Planters Corporation, *1972 Annual Report*, p. 3.

[144]*Ibid.*, p. 2.

[145]Union Planters Corporation, *1972 Financial Statements*, p. 2.

[146]*Ibid.*, pp. 1, 2.

[147]*Ibid.*

[148]*Ibid.*, p. 2.

[149]*Ibid.*, p. 10.

[150]Union Planters Corporation, *1973 Annual Report*, pp. 5, 28.

[151]*Ibid.*, pp. 5-6.

[152]Bruce Sankey, "President Resigns at Union Planters," *The Commercial Appeal*, November 28, 1973. No page number on clipping.

[153]*1973 Annual Report, op.cit., supra*, n. 150, p. 6.

[154]Sankey, *op.cit., supra*, n. 152.

[155]"Ex-Chief of UP Takes New Post," *The Commercial Appeal*, January 24, 1974. No page number on clipping.

[156]*1973 Annual Report, op.cit., supra*, n. 150, p. 6.

[157]Jerry L. Robbins, "Union Planters Says 'House in Order' for Future After Reorganization at Top," *The Commercial Appeal*, November 28, 1973, p. 29.

[158]*1973 Annual Report, op.cit., supra*, n. 150, p. 6.

[159]"No. 3 Official Resigns Union Planters Position," *The Commercial Appeal*, December 20, 1973. No page number on clipping.

[160]*1973 Annual Report, op.cit., supra*, n. 150, pp. 3-6.

[161]*Ibid.*, p. 22.

[162]*Ibid.*, p. 14.

[163]*Ibid.*, p. 15.

[164]*Ibid.*, p. 6.

[165]*Ibid.*, p. 13.

[166]Conversation with James A. Gurley.

[167]*Ibid.*

[168]*Ibid.*

[169]*Ibid.*

[170]"Webb Picked to Guide UP Bank," *Press Scimitar*, January 10, 1974, p. 1.

[171]"Hard-Driving Matthews Turns Profit at Shaken Union Planters," *American Banker*, February 21, 1978, p. 2.

[172]Conversation with William M. Matthews.

[173]*Ibid.*

[174]*Ibid.*

[175]"Insurance Firm Buys 100 North Main," *The Commercial Appeal*, July 11, 1974. No page number on clipping.

[176]"Real Estate Losses Hit UP," *American Banker*, August 12, 1974.

[177]"UP Board Chairman Resigns: Trippeer, New President, Says Losses Now 'Over'," *Press Scimitar*, October 18, 1974. No page number on clipping.

[178]*Ibid.*

[179]*Ibid.*

[180]James C. Treadway, Jr., "Securities Exchange Commission Enforcement Techniques: Expanding An Exotic Ancillary Relief," *The Washington And Lee Law Review*, XXXII, (No. 3, 1975), pp. 660-663.

[181]Conversations with William M. Matthews.

[182]*Ibid.*

[183]"Probe is Linked to Bank Losses," *The Commercial Appeal*, November 5, 1974. No page number on clipping.

[184]Tom Jones, "Memphis Bank Sues CBS, Inc., Over Stax Loan," *Press Scimitar*, November 14, 1974. No page number on clipping.

[185]"Union Planters Skips Payout for First Time Since 1928," *Wall Street Journal*, December 12, 1974. No page number on clipping.

[186]"Jury Resumes Inquiry into UP Bank Affairs," *The Commercial Appeal*, December 12, 1974. No page number on clipping.

[187]"Employees Told About Bank Probe," *Press Scimitar*, December 12, 1974. No page number on clipping.

[188]*Ibid.*

[189]Michael Lollar, "Two Indicted In Bank Embezzlements," *The Commercial Appeal*, December 13, 1974, p. 42. Richard Powelson, "Notification of His Indictment Received on Wedding Night," *Press Scimitar*, December 13, 1974. No page number on clipping.

[190]Union Planters Corporation, *1974 Annual Report*, pp. 24-27.

[191]Forrest Laws, "UP Board Chairman Shuns Role of Social Leader," *Press Scimitar*. No page number on clipping, but the early part of January 1975 is presumed.

[192]Bruce Sankey, "Matthews' Decision-Making Ability is Chief Asset," *The Commercial Appeal*, January 19, 1975. No page number on clipping.

[193]*1974 Annual Report, op.cit., supra*, n. 190, pp. 5,7.

[194]"How to Deal with Bad News Constructively a'la Union Planters," *Senior Bank Executives Report*, Vol. 10, No. 4, February 19, 1975.

[195]*Press Scimitar*, June 26, 1975. No page number on clipping.

[196]"Georgia Executive Made UP Corp. Vice Chairman," *The Commercial Appeal*, July 1, 1975. No page number on clipping.

[197]"How a Memphis Bank Stopped its Crime Wave," *Business Week*, October 27, 1975, pp. 63-64.

[198]*Ibid.*, p. 64.

[199]*Ibid.*

[200]Union Planters Corporation, *1975 Annual Report*, p. 7.

[201]"Annie Will Compete with Live Tellers in UP Innovation," *The Commercial Appeal*, June 27, 1976. No page number on clipping.

[202]"30 Stores to Utilize UP's Annie," *The Commercial Appeal*, September 19, 1976. No page number on clipping.

[203]Bruce Sankey, "UP Pioneers Pension-Profit Plan," *The Commercial Appeal*, October 13, 1976. No page number on clipping.

[204]"Union Planters To Begin Honoring BankAmericard," *The Commercial Appeal*, October 17, 1976. No page number on clipping.

[205]"Banker Says Memphis Needs Outside Planning," *The Commercial Appeal*, April 12, 1977. No page number on clipping.

[206]Lewis Nolan, "Bill-Paying by Telephone Will be Added to UP Services in Fall," *The Commercial Appeal*, June 8, 1977. No page number on clipping.

[207]*1974 Annual Report, op.cit., supra*, n. 190, p. 5.

[208]*Ibid.*, p. 6.

[209]*Ibid.*

[210]*Ibid.*, pp. 22, 24-25.

[211]*1975 Annual Report, op.cit., supra*, n. 200, p. 2.

[212]*Ibid.*, pp. 16, 22-23.

[213]Union Planters Corporation, *1976 Annual Report*, pp. 2, 8, 9.

[214]"UP Buying Mortgage Loans as $2.5 Million Venture," *The Commercial Appeal*, August 10, 1976. No page number on clipping.

[215]*1976 Annual Report, op. cit., supra*, n. 213, pp. 32-35, 44, 52, 53.

[216]Union Planters Corporation, *1977 Annual Report*, pp. 2, 3, 23, 29, 30, 37.

[217]Union Planters Corporation, *1978 Annual Report*, p. 3.

[218]*Ibid.*, pp. 3, 32.

[219]Union Planters Corporation, *1979 Annual Report*, pp. 3, 18, 19, 25.

[220]"UP Tops State Banks In Profitability," *The Commercial Appeal*, July 18, 1980, p. B-14.

SELECTED BIBLIOGRAPHY

"Alexander Advises Bankers to Drop 'Deep Blue Glasses' and Lend Money," November 8, 1934, no publication indicated.

American Banker, September 8, 1969.

"Annie Will Compete with Live Tellers in UP Innovation," *The Commercial Appeal*, June 27, 1976.

"Bank Earnings Dip," *The Commercial Appeal*, April 14, 1972.

"Bank Seeks Change," *The Commercial Appeal*, May 2, 1972.

"Banker Says Memphis Needs Outside Planning," *The Commercial Appeal*, April 12, 1977.

"Bankers Expect Growth Despite Economic Conditions," *Press Scimitar*, January 13, 1971.

Banks, Lucille Webb. "Insurance Firm Gave Memphis Bank Birth," *The Memphis Press*, March 15, 1928.

Beldon Associates. *A Study of the Banking Market in Memphis, March-April 1974* (Dallas: 1974).

"Branch Banking Today Part of Modern Trend of Financial Service," *Daily News*, September 12, 1969.

Cole, James. "Bankers Expect More Bullishness," *The Commercial Appeal*, January 9, 1972.

Colman, Robert F. *Linear Programming and Cash Management/Cash Alpha* (Cambridge, Mass.: The M.I.T. Press, 1968).

The Commercial Appeal, January 15, 1952.

Conversations with James A. Gurley by author.

Conversations with William M. Matthews by author.

Dunn, Ed. "Chamber of Commerce Begins 'Believe in Memphis' Drive," *Press Scimitar*, November 21, 1972.

"Employees Told About Bank Probe," *Press Scimitar*. December 12, 1974.

"Ex-Chief of UP Takes New Post," *The Commercial Appeal*, January 24, 1974.

Farrington, William M. *Address to the Stockholders of the Union & Planters Bank of Memphis*, September 26, 1874.

Finance: The Magazine of Money (October, 1969).

"Georgia Executive Made UP Corp. Vice Chairman," *The Commercial Appeal*, July 1, 1975.

Goyer, C. W., et al. "To the Stockholders of Union & Planters Bank of Memphis." A response to W. M. Farrington's remarks regarding the bank's actions, in *Address to the Stockholders of the Union and Planters Bank of Memphis* (October 8, 1874).

"Hard-Driving Matthews Turns Profit at Shaken Union Planters," *American Banker*, February 21, 1978.

Harrison, C. Bennett. "What are the Prospects for 1971?" *Mid-Continent Banker*, January, 1971.

Heflin, John J. (As told to a staff reporter). "Memphis Booms—Clearings Tell the Story," Sec. V, *The Commercial Appeal*, January 20, 1952.

"How to Deal with Bad News Constructively a 'la Union Planters," *Senior Bank Executives Report*, Vol. 10, No. 4., February 19, 1975.

"How a Memphis Bank Stopped Its Crime Wave," *Business Week*, October 27, 1975.

"Insurance Firm Buys 100 North Main," *The Commercial Appeal*, July 11, 1974.

Jones, Tom. "Memphis Bank Sues CBS, Inc. Over Stax Loan," *Press Scimitar*, November 14, 1974.

"Jury Resumes Inquiry into UP Bank Affairs," *The Commercial Appeal*, December 12, 1974.

Laws, Forrest. "UP Board Chairman Shuns Role of Social Leader," *Press Scimitar*, No date given.

Lollar, Michael. "Two Indicted in Bank Embezzlements," *The Commercial Appeal*, December 13, 1974.

McFerrin, John Berry. *Caldwell & Company: A Southern Financial, Empire* Vanderbilt University Press: 1969.

McKelvey, Rosemary. "Union Planters is 100 Year Old!" *Mid-Continent Banker*, August, 1969.

Meanley, Tom. "UP's New Head Finds Phone a Busy Thing!" *Press Scimitar*, January 15, 1955.

Memphis Chamber of Commerce. *Memphis: A Short Historical Sketch with a Summary of Important Dates* (Memphis).

(Memphis) *Press Scimitar*, June 26, 1975.

Michael, Thomas, " 'Retiring' Vance Alexander Has No Plans for Leaving," *The Commercial Appeal,* January 11, 1963.

Mid-Continent Banker, August, 1969.

"No. 3 Official Resigns Union Planters Position," *The Commercial Appeal*, December 20, 1973.

Nolan, Lewis. "Bill Paying by Telephone Will be Added to UP Services in Fall," *The Commercial Appeal*, June 8, 1977.

Peat, Marwick, Mitchell & Co. "Letter Addressed to Mr. Harrison," November 1, 1971.

Pollard, David. "Understanding & Patience Typify New UP Board Chief," *The Commercial Appeal*, February 11, 1968.

Powelson, Richard. "Notification of His Indictment Received on Wedding Night," *Press Scimitar*, December 13, 1974.

"Probe is Linked to Bank Losses," *The Commercial Appeal*, November 5, 1974.

"Real Estate Losses Hit UP," *American Banker*, August 12, 1974.

"Remodeling Program Fosters Progressive Image," *Mid-Continent Banker*, December, 1972.

"Retiring UP Bank Official Praised for Long Service." Worn newspaper clipping found in bank's archives which does not show publisher or date.

Robbins, Jerry L. "Union Planters Says 'House in Order' for Future After Reorganization at Top," *Press Scimitar*, November 28, 1973.

Sankey, Bruce. "Matthews' Decision-Making Ability is Chief Asset," *The Commercial Appeal*, January 19, 1975.

Sankey, Bruce. "President Resigns at Union Planters," *The Commercial Appeal*, November 28, 1973.

Sankey, Bruce. "UP Pioneers Pension-Profit Plan," *The Commercial Appeal*, October 13, 1976.

"A Short History of the Union Planters National Bank & Trust Company." An unpublished two-page document found in the bank's archives.

"Signs Point to Growth of Mid-South Economy," *Press Scimitar*, May 4, 1972.

Silver, Louis. "Banks Grow Up, Base Interest Rate on Own Area," *The Commercial Appeal*, January 13, 1972.

" 'Stay South,' Advises Alexander." No author or publication cited.

Talley, Robert. "Long Pillar of City, Mid-South Historic Union Planters Bank Will Start New Era This Week," *The Commercial Appeal*, Sec. II, April 27, 1952.

"30 Stores to Utilize UP's Annie," *The Commercial Appeal*, September 19, 1976.

Treadway, James C., Jr. "Securities Exchange Commission Enforcement Techniques: Expanding an Exotic Ancillary Relief," *The Washington And Lee Law Review*, Vo. XXXII (1975).

"UP Buying Mortgage Loans as $2.5 Million Venture," *The Commercial Appeal*, August 10, 1976.

"UP Chairman Resigns: Trippeer, New President, Says Losses Now 'Over'," *Press Scimitar*, October 18, 1974.

Union & Planters Bank & Trust Company. *The Story of a Memphis Institution: 1869-1919* (1919).

"Union Planters To Begin Honoring BankAmericard," *The Commercial Appeal*, October 17, 1976.

Union Planters Corporation. *Annual Reports.* 1972-1979.

"Union Planters National Bank: Corporate Background." An unpublished four-page report found in archives.

Union Planters National Bank of Memphis. *Annual Reports to Stockholders.* 1943-1979.

"Union Planters Skips Payout for First Time Since 1928," *Wall Street Journal*, December 12, 1974.

Union Planters National Bank & Trust Co. "Souvenir of the Sixtieth Birthday of the Union Planters National Bank & Trust Co." 1869-1929. Unpublished booklet.

Unpublished summary of information reported in Memphis newspapers regarding Union Planters shortening its name.

"Wall Street Transcript," April 10, 1972.

"Webb Picked to Guide UP Bank," *Press Scimitar*, January 10, 1974.

"Young UP President Sees Gains in Year," *The Commercial Appeal*, Sec. III, October 11, 1970.

INDEX